* * * *
The Peppermint Train

Edgar E. Stern

The Peppermint Train

University Press of Florida
*Gainesville
Tallahassee
Tampa
Boca Raton
Pensacola
Orlando
Miami
Jacksonville*

Journey to a German-Jewish Childhood

Copyright 1992 by the Board of
Regents of the State of Florida
All rights reserved
Printed in the U.S. on recycled, acid-
free paper ∞

Library of Congress Cataloging in
Publication Data are available on last
printed page of book.

The University Press of Florida is the
scholarly publishing agency of the
State University System of Florida,
comprised of Florida A & M
University, Florida Atlantic University,
Florida International University,
Florida State University, University of
Central Florida, University of Florida,
University of North Florida, University of South Florida, and University of
West Florida.

University Presses of Florida
15 Northwest 15th Street
Gainesville, FL 32611

Frontispiece: Egon on his four-wheeler
with his grandfather watching.

Contents

	Author's Note	vii
	Acknowledgments	ix
1.	A Torn Connection	1
2.	Speyer	5
3.	My Childhood Village	15
4.	"Juden Verboten"	23
5.	What Did Egon Do Wrong?	29
6.	My Chocolate Farewell	35
7.	Edgar	40
8.	Yesterday's Fears	49
9.	Another Side of My Father	56
10.	A Bridge to Home	64
11.	"We Were So Close, Your Family and Mine"	79
12.	A Cathedral, a Synagogue, a T-shirt	91
13.	We Are All Born Naked	97
14.	Looking for Redemption	112
15.	The Holocaust on Our Bread	140
16.	"So Attached Was He Here"	153
17.	Reclaiming Boyhood Trains	163
18.	Noble Man	171
19.	The Horrible Ambivalence	184
20.	Don't They Know We Can't Forget?	191
21.	*Das Pfefferminzbähnel*	203
22.	Dachau	210
23.	I Know Now	214
	Photographs	127-39

Author's Note

I HAVE reported the experiences in this memoir as honestly and candidly as possible. Since many of the events and conversations are described in detail, a word is in order about how I have recalled them.

I began work on *The Peppermint Train* immediately after my visit to Germany in 1983. I reported that trip, and the events preceding it, from recent memory, detailed journal notes, and photographs. Upon my return, I tape-recorded most conversations related to the trip, as well as my discussions with others regarding their feelings about returning to Germany. During my 1985 visit, I used my tape recorder consistently, supplemented by detailed daily notes. I reconstructed dialogues with my wife and son with their assistance.

I believe I possess a good ability to observe and remember scenes, human interactions and my own feelings. This skill has been sharpened by my professional training and experience in social work, psychotherapy, and sociology. Moreover, to ensure authenticity, I conducted numerous interviews and researched various sources, including Holocaust literature, historical records and family documents.

Regarding childhood memories, no author can honestly claim precise accuracy. I do believe, however, that my early recollections, including the dialogue, are close replications of original events. One or two minor characters from this period probably represent composite memories.

I have changed some names of persons to protect privacy. Also, when the real names of two individuals were the same, I modified them to avoid confusion for the reader.

Acknowledgments

I WOULD LIKE to give recognition to the individuals and organizations without whose help this book would probably not have reached publication.

First, thanks to my editorial consultant, Bibi Wein, who helped me not only with her technical expertise but with her understanding and patience.

Credit goes to the many individuals referred to in the text for the interviews and information they provided. Special gratitude goes to Otto Galle and Christian Rosskopf. My appreciation goes to Norman Sassler, who read the manuscript critically and contributed to my insights about Jewish history and the Holocaust.

Thanks go to Janice Booker, who in her writing classes at the University of Pennsylvania not only helped me with technical advice but also nurtured the early stages of my book. For contributing their time by reading and commenting on drafts of the book, my appreciation goes to Kim Fendrick, Barry Fox, Josey Fisher, James Muller, Harry Neuman, Joan Speck. My thanks go also to Hanna Silver, who checked my German-English translations.

I want to acknowledge several institutions where I conducted my literature research for the book: the Leo Baeck Institute, the Cinnaminson Branch and the Main Branch of the Burlington County Library, Gratz College, and the Van Pelt Library of the University of Pennsylvania.

My appreciation goes to my publisher for scrupulous attention to the editorial quality of this book.

Finally, many thanks to my wife and children, for reading and commenting on the numerous drafts, and for their emotional support throughout my work on the manuscript.

* * * * *

I

A Torn Connection

ONE NIGHT DURING the spring of 1983, I had a dream—a bad dream, a nightmare.

In my wooded backyard a man was racing around on a monstrous motorcycle. He was a man who "could do everything and stopped at nothing." He whirred his huge cycle right through the trunks of the trees. The trees all fell down. A little boy in the yard was playing with a lizard, and the man-who-stopped-at-nothing plunged his machine into the innocent little animal and its blood spurted into the boy's face.

When I got over my fright and tried to understand the dream, I thought of the wonderful woods where I was raised in Germany. And I thought of the German woods where Hitler's monstrous machinery destroyed millions of people. I was spared while others shed blood. The blood is on me nonetheless.

* * * * *

Some weeks before that dream, on a cold February night, I was sitting in my living room listening to Andrés Segovia on my stereo. The sweet sounds of the great classical guitarist, hero and inspiration for my own playing efforts, could not shut out what my wife and I had talked about earlier that evening. Milly and I had been discussing our plans to visit Germany.

I was nine years old when my family fled the Nazis in 1936. Now, forty-seven years later, I found myself thinking about my German childhood, and fond memories began to surface. I longed to go back, to look up the scenes of those fond memories, and to visit a cousin, Lore, whom I hadn't seen since I was a little boy. The idea had first entered my mind in the late 1970s and blossomed into an actual plan after my father died in 1979. "What better way to use some of my inheritance," I said at the time, "than to look up my roots."

But on this cold night in 1983 we began discussing our serious doubts. "It's our twenty-fifth anniversary this year and we want a grand vacation, not a painful one," Milly had pointed out.

Turning off the stereo because I could not enjoy Segovia that night, I glumly recalled that Lore's father, my father's brother Willie, had been in a concentration camp. He was lucky and survived. His wife, my Aunt Helene, was not Jewish, and Jews in mixed marriages weren't deported en masse until the last year of the war.

My father had corresponded with Willie and Helene after the war. So had I on occasion. Uncle Willie had sent my son, Walt, a German zither for his bar mitzvah. That was eleven years ago and Willie had died since then. I didn't know if Helene was still alive.

Some of my father's other siblings were not as lucky. Arthur was killed by the Germans. I never knew him well, but I remembered Anna and her two daughters, Lydia and Gertrude. They were sent to Auschwitz. Aunt Anna and Lydia were gassed. Gertrude survived and eventually went to Sweden.

As I sat on the sofa, I felt a cold draft on my feet from a leaky soffit under the window, a leak which I had meant to fix for a long time. I shuddered, but not just from the cold. Terrible thoughts chilled my soul. I had read lots of books and seen movies about Hitler and about the Holocaust, and I had taught my three children to "never forget." And now, in 1983, I asked myself, Should I really go back to Germany? Can I?

Lore had just written how happy she was that I was coming. I couldn't disappoint her again. In 1980, Milly and I had registered to attend a social work conference in Germany and planned to visit Lore. We had changed our minds because the conference cost too much and left us little free time. We went to Israel instead. Milly had preferred going there, anyhow.

In 1982, our son, Walt, visited Lore while on a European trip with his senior university class. Lore was so delighted, he told us, and he was enchanted with what he saw of Germany. "I'd like to go back some time," he said.

But it wasn't really Lore's feelings that spurred me to go ahead with the plans. It was some need deep inside me that made me want to go back to Germany this year—something I couldn't fully explain. My time to go back had come. Something stirring inside me needed to be satisfied. Like the leak in the soffit which I would fix this year, I perhaps needed to fix something about my past.

As I paced about my living room, restlessly musing, I stopped in front of a large painting on the wall. It was a charcoal and watercolor picture of a narrow cobblestone street, really more like an alley, lined by rows of old houses, with wooden handcarts and wagons standing at the curb of tiny sidewalks and a few people walking to and fro. At the center of this quiet scene was a tall church steeple with a cupola, resting against a peaceful cloud drifting in a gray-blue sky. An inscription on the painting identified the street as "Johannisgasse." And looking at that scene obliterated my churning thoughts and calmed me.

Johannisgasse was in the old section of Speyer, the small German city where I was born and where I spent most of my first nine years. Somewhere on that cobblestone street I went to my first school, I recalled. Suddenly I wanted to know exactly where that school was—up the street from the church or at the other end?

I remembered riding my bike to school and leaving it with people in a house across the street. My parents were paying for that. But one day I overheard my parents saying that those people wouldn't deal with Jews any more. I'd have to leave my bicycle in our store on the way to school and walk the rest of the way.

I was struck with an irony: I had had that picture of Speyer on my wall for years. In fact, as far as I could recall, the picture had hung in every apartment my parents lived in, probably since they first arrived in America. I walked over to a bookcase to look at a souvenir plate depicting a view of the Rhine River at Speyer. It filled me with warmth. Then I looked toward my entrance foyer, at a pen-and-ink drawing of an ancient German city-gate with a picturesque clock-tower. It was the Altpörtel, Speyer's old main entrance. Even in my office, I realized, I had a painting of a peaceful German pastoral scene, one that had also hung in my parents' home for years.

I had passed these lovely scenes of my boyhood day after day for much of my life, and it now struck me that I had never thought about them much. And when I did, it was for a moment, as if I had to quickly wipe the nostalgia away. But now the scenes came into sharp focus, and longing flowed in my veins. I realized that for all these years those pictures implicitly kept alive my connection with my homeland.

As I went to bed, I felt a lump in my throat and an undefined fear in my chest, and my mind churned once more with doubts about going back to Germany. But I longed to see Speyer again.

* * * * *

2

Speyer

When Milly came upstairs I asked her, "Did I ever talk to you much about Speyer?"

"No," she replied. "You never talked about your childhood at all. When I'd ask you questions you'd either ignore them or pass over them very lightly."

That's odd, I thought, considering all the therapy I've had. Even odder considering the fact that as a therapist I spend a good deal of time helping others talk about *their* childhoods.

"Those pictures of Germany hanging on my walls all these years," I said, "it's as if I never really saw them. Yet, at times I'd think a little about Speyer. And sometimes Schwegenheim and Mannheim and places my mother used to mention, like Karlsruhe." Like fleeting excursions into the past, I reflected.

"You were eight, weren't you, when you left?" Milly asked.

"Almost nine," I said. "In fact, I'll never forget my birthday that year. We'd been here for ten days. My parents, Aunt Selma, Uncle Eugene, and cousin Bernie—his name was Gerd then—were in the kitchen. The adults were talking serious business—like getting jobs. Then Uncle Eugene remarked that it was my birthday. I waited sort of expectantly, and finally my father said,

'We can't do much this year.' He handed me a nickel, and tears came to my eyes."

"Well, a nickel was worth a lot more in those days," Milly noted.

I left the room to turn up the heat. Even our new storm windows couldn't keep out the frigid wind that night. When I came back to bed, I continued, "I never realized how little I talked about my boyhood. I don't recall my parents talking much about Germany either. Did they ever talk to you about it?"

Milly said my mother used to tell some anecdotes about me and my parents and grandparents and occasionally about other relatives. "But those were the same kind of family stories any woman tells here daughter-in-law. Oh, I know from conversations that your parents had a big millinery store there in Speyer, but they never talked in any detail about their lives in Germany."

"Not even about Speyer," I said. "Despite the pictures on their walls. I guess they must have pushed it out of their minds. They lost a good business there, and a good home."

I was about to say that they lost a beautiful homeland, that Germany is a beautiful country with lovely woods, the Rhine, the villages. But the words stuck in my throat. Images came to mind of my father's relatives in the concentration camps, of horrible scenes from films I had seen and from the books I had studied about Hitler and the Holocaust.

Suddenly I had a sensation that I was smelling human flesh—from Hitler's ovens. I threw the blankets off, jumped out of bed, and stood there shaking. "Six million Jews!" I blurted. "And millions of others they killed!"

Milly sat up, watching me pace the floor and listening to my strident tones. "How can I go back there? How can I face that place? And those people? It's no wonder I've waited all these years. I've pushed a lot out of my mind. It wasn't just money that kept me from going back before this, and in 1980 it wasn't just your pushing for Israel that kept me from Germany."

"Ed," Milly began, "I never wanted to hold you back from seeing your birthplace and where you spent your childhood. I'm sure it's very important to you, maybe more than either of us have realized. But I'm not keen on going to that *Deutschland!* I want you to go, see your cousin, even enjoy yourself. But frankly, Ed, I don't want to spend a nickel more than I have to there."

Her words stung. They scared me. I was curious about why she felt so strongly. She was born in America. Her parents weren't German, and they had come to America long before World War II. They had, though, suffered pogroms in Russia. Milly's words stung because she had expressed the negative feelings I felt but could not quite admit. They scared me because I could see it now: me dragging Milly around Germany against her will—what stress!

Milly soon fell asleep, but I went downstairs. I took my guitar and began to strum. After a few minutes, I found myself humming a line of a German song, *"Muss i denn, muss i denn zum Städtle hinaus, Städtle hinaus."* It was one of my favorite folk songs. Gradually my attention was drawn to the Johannisgasse painting on the wall. I put the guitar down and closed my eyes.

A place in Speyer called the Postplatz appeared in my mind. It was fuzzy, but I saw just enough that I could have drawn a rough picture of it. I could have drawn other parts of Speyer too, just as, I now realized, I'd had the impulse to do during previous imaginary excursions over the years. It's interesting, I reflected, that I never so much as picked up a pencil. As I returned to bed, I wondered what Johannisgasse and the rest of Speyer would look like now.

The next morning I woke up eager to go about my present life and put the past aside. Outside, there was a thin cover of newly fallen snow, and as I brushed the snow off the car, thoughts about my childhood pressed back into mind. How lucky I was that we had wealthy relatives in America who brought us over here. Then, as I drove slowly on the slippery streets, past white lawns, a vision came to mind of a small frozen lake. It was near my home in rural Speyer. Children were ice-skating on the lake—or was it a pond? When I was old enough I was allowed to go there alone, but I'd just stand watching because I couldn't skate. It made me feel bad, but I slid around on my shoes, and once in a while someone on skates or on a sled asked me to give them a push. That made me feel good. Even now, a smile came to my face.

* * * * *

I was born in a hospital in Speyer on July 19, 1927. My parents and my mother's parents lived in the village of Schwegenheim a few miles away. My mother's name was Elsa, my father's Otto. They named me Egon.

I didn't know exactly when we moved from Schwegenheim to Speyer. My parents opened a store there in 1927 or 1928, so I figured we must have moved around then. I also knew I was with my grandparents a lot during that part of my life. I'd been told that they virtually raised me.

Speyer was a small city of about 25,000 people, in the Pfalz region in southwestern Germany. It was a charming place on the Rhine, with cobbled alleys, a wide main street with many little stores, many old churches, and woods all around.

A few days after my talk with Milly, I looked Speyer up in a travel guide, which described it as a very old community that had originated as an early Celtic settlement at least a thousand years before Christ. Although it was now a major cultural and commercial hub of 50,000 people, it had, according to the book, retained its ancient charm.

Once again I started drawing a mental map: my home in a rural area about half a mile from the center of town, the pond, cobblestone streets and alleys, and the memorable main square of the town, the Postplatz, which literally means "Post Place." On one side of the square stood the large Postamt, the post office. On the adjoining side stood the ancient tower-gate with its big clock, the Altpörtel, and on a third side were several stores. One of those stores was on a corner of a narrow cobblestone street which fed into the square. That was my parents' millinery shop.

I pictured myself standing in front of our store looking at the old Altpörtel to my right, then turning my head and seeing the gray ornate Postamt across the square. Then I turned around and looked down the narrow cobbled street, wondering if I would ever again walk or bicycle down that street to my former home. "Wouldn't it be interesting," I thought, "if I could rent a bike when I'm there . . ." but the thought quickly faded as a lump formed in my throat.

The next time I studied the travel book, I imagined myself standing on the other side of the Altpörtel, looking down the main street lined with many stores in charming old buildings and at the end, in the distance, the imposing cathedral—the Dom—that was, and still is, Speyer's most famous landmark.

If, as a child, I ever knew the significance of that huge church, I had long forgotten it. The travel guide said that the Dom dated back to A.D. 1030 and that it is the largest Romanesque church in Europe. Reading those words reawakened an old glow. Speyer citizens were proud of their Dom. The travel guide also said German emperors were buried in it. That made me somewhat uneasy, but at dinner I said to Milly, "I was reading about Speyer and think I want to see the Dom again. It's a famous cathedral. There are German emperors buried there."

"German emperors," she said, mockingly. "Spike-helmeted men who made wars."

Her remark illuminated my own uneasiness. "And Hitler became an emperor," I said. "He didn't wear a helmet but he took after that whole bunch."

I jutted out my chin and with a staunch jaw contrived my best guttural German accent: "Empperrrors offf Cherrmanie. *Oi, mein Gott!*" I added, as Milly gave forth with characteristic hearty laughter and my daughter Karen giggled.

But I knew then that I would never again look at the Dom with pride, nor perhaps even the enthusiasm of a sightseer. Yet, the sight of that cathedral was an almost daily occurrence for the young boy, Egon. I still felt in my nostrils the delicious woods around it that spread back to the Rhine and over to the fields where I lived.

Somewhere in those woods was a spot called the Messplatz, the fairground where my grandfather used to take me, where I used to scamper around gathering walnuts and chestnuts under the tall trees. Opa rode a large three-wheeler because he was handicapped. He walked with canes, which he had carved himself. When I was little he would tie string around my waist to keep me from getting too far away from him. When we'd get home he'd put some chestnuts on the wood stove, and oh how I loved to smell them roasting on the fire and to eat the tasty foods my grandmother cooked with them.

* * * * *

The more I thought about the trip, the more I realized I still had attachments to my German background. But I also became increasingly aware of my conflicted feelings, even about the language.

Over the years, I spoke German occasionally with relatives and friends. When our three children were young, I taught them German words and phrases. But in recent years the opportunity to speak German had become rare, and I got rusty. Now, I felt the urge to brush up. Lore and her husband knew no English and not only did I want to be able to speak to them, but I wanted to learn a few things about our family and the war. Besides, I might be talking to other Germans.

I'd always gotten some pleasure from speaking German. Even in recent years I'd amused Milly and the children by breaking into a German accent. And I'd utter German expletives, for fun or in moments of frustration: "*Verrücktes Ding,*" "*Verdammt,*" "*Schweinehund.*"

Also, I had for years made fun by intoning my own made-up guttural nonsense words or phrases—in the shower, while mowing the lawn—like "*Undiflegen,*" "*schmingi.*" My father used to make up words like that. But I outdid him. I'd create sentences that sounded like a German version of pig latin: "*Schrackdich foden und die Mihuden.*"

I had one favorite expression that was real German, though: "*Ja hat er gesagt! Und dann ist er kaputt gegangen.*" It would resound through the house, sometimes bringing echoes from Milly and the kids, especially from Debbie, my older daughter, who liked that one in particular. When they asked what it meant, I'd explain, "I think it means, 'Yes, he said! And then he went broken.' I learned it in New York as a kid, from the owner of a grocery store where I worked. He just burst out with it once in a while out of the clear blue. Maybe he was worried about going broke."

And I now recalled that as a teenager in America, while hiking with my German-Jewish buddies, we would break into German marching cadence, "*Einz, zwei, drei, vier . . . links, rechts, links, rechts.*" That was during the middle of the war, it suddenly struck me—while the Germans were slaughtering the millions!

I discussed my trip one day with a colleague who had come to the United States not long before and who had a thick German accent. I launched into German, and was talking away when suddenly it occurred to me that I'd been forced out of Germany. Should I be enjoying this language? It was as if I wanted to repossess my heritage while at the same time rejecting it. I'd speak German and suddenly there would arise in me a hesitation, a reluctance, and at times a revulsion.

On another day I recalled that over the years I'd often sing German folk songs, that at family parties the German relatives and friends would join in, and that I taught the songs to my kids. That afternoon, I was counseling a German woman who had come to the United States after the war. I felt an instant emotional attraction to her German accent and blonde hair. But quickly, I backed my mind away. I wanted to ask the woman what part of Germany she was from and to tell her I was born there. But I didn't. More urgently, I felt like asking, "What did *you* do to Jews during the war?"

Somehow, Germany did enter our conversation. She said it was a beautiful country. She even went on to say, "It was a shame what happened years ago." She didn't like to talk about it, she added.

I asked her if she would like to go back to live in Germany.

No, she liked it here. "It's not perfect, but no place is. But I often think of Germany," she added. "In fact, I think of it as *my* Germany."

"I know that feeling so well!" I wanted to reply, but I looked away. Germany was not *my* Germany any more.

My encounter with that woman brought my mixed emotions into focus. "I don't know how I'll face Germans in Germany—the real ones," I told Milly that evening, "especially those that were old enough to be in the war."

"And how will we feel sitting in a restaurant," Milly said, "thinking that a Jew murderer could be sitting next to us?"

* * * * *

But as more negative feelings about Germany surfaced, so did more fond memories.

My home was on a dirt road in the outskirts of Speyer. To my recollection there was only one other house near ours, on a farm across the way. Complete rural bliss, it was to me. However, a conversation with my Aunt Selma refreshed my memory about a small factory next door to us. "Didn't they used to make things out of wood?" I recalled.

"Furniture," she replied. Then I remembered that there was a fire in that factory when I was a little boy.

Our apartment was on the second floor of a three-story house. I even remembered the layout of the rooms. Also, I had a faint recollection of a room on the third floor, in which I used to sleep. Since Aunt Selma had lived with us for a while, I asked her about it.

"Don't know," she grunted.

Aunt Selma, now seventy-seven, had not been well and had been hospitalized twice recently. Today she periodically coughed, grunted, groaned, often saying "don't know" or not answering at all. I felt bad that she was deteriorating so. I always felt close to her, despite the feuds she and my parents had had over the years. In some ways she was like a second mother to me.

I didn't want to push her too much today, but her son Bernie and his wife urged her to keep telling me things about Germany. "It's good exercise for your mind," they told her. They also reminded me that my visits always cheered her up. So I kept asking her questions.

I got her to laugh when I recalled that we used to have chickens and geese in the yard and that it was quite a sight to see Grandmother catch a goose and force-feed it. She'd hold it by the neck, pry its mouth open and stuff corn down its throat till no more would go in. That's how they fattened the poor animal up.

"And, Aunt Selma, do you remember the egg house?" I chuckled.

She didn't answer.

"Don't you remember?"

"Don't know," she grunted.

I recalled it for her. It was a little chicken coop, attached to the corner of the house, no bigger than a large dog house probably. I used to crawl in, pick up the eggs, and hand them out to my grandmother.

When I got home that night, I began flipping through my parent's old family album, trying to find a picture of that part of the yard. I stopped instead at a photo of myself with a playmate on the potato field of his farm across the street from our house. His name was Klaus. We must have been about four. Klaus, with blunt-cut blond hair, dressed in a clean knit polo and short pants over long stockings, stood calmly looking into the camera; I, with a thick shock of curly blond hair, was half crouched, balancing myself in ankle-high shoes, my hands on muddy knees, mischievous eyes peering from a dirty face into the lens. I chuckled at the picture.

As I looked at the photos of Klaus, of his house, his family, I became conscious of feeling no particular connection and recalling nothing concrete about him. His name, I thought, must have stayed with me only from overhearing my family's occasional references to Speyer. Then, I seemed to recall them saying that after Hitler came into power, Klaus stopped playing with me, and that he ultimately joined the Hitler Youth organization. As I looked at him on the potato field, I wondered, why in the world would such a young boy become a Nazi?

There was also a photo of another playmate, Helga, whose family lived in the first-floor apartment of our house. We were seated on my rocking horse. We must have been around six. My rocking horse looked like a real pony. Its hide was a very dark brown or black, and it had a white mane on a lifelike head with glass eyes that looked real, teeth in an open mouth straining as if it were in a gallop, and a gray tail of real horsehair. Helga was seated in front, holding on to the pony's neck, while I, with feet in the stirrups, was embracing her from behind. We must have been trying hard to smile for the camera, showing missing teeth, while trying to keep the horse still for the photo.

Helga stopped playing with me too.

I didn't look at the album for quite a while after that—maybe because of the painful questions it raised. What did Klaus and Helga do to Jews during the war? How could a chasm between fond memories and resentment be bridged? Should I even try?

For a while, I did stop trying. My warmth toward Speyer receded, and a gray haze once again enveloped Johannisgasse, the Postplatz, the Dom, the cobbled streets, the woods, the chestnuts, the house, the pond. I wasn't sure if I could or should lift that haze again.

Nonetheless, it lifted on its own. The memories kept coming back. One of them was about two bridges. A pontoon bridge crossed the Rhine somewhere at the edge of the woods behind the Dom. Very faintly, I remembered there were railroad tracks on it. Then, more clearly, I recalled a train ride across that bridge—the time when my mother and grandmother took me to Heidelberg.

The other bridge came to symbolize all of my torn connections with Speyer and Germany. About 1934, a new bridge across the Rhine was begun. Its train tracks would pass only a few hundred feet from my house. The embankment went up, then a trestle was laid over my street, and a small station platform was erected. We'd climb up the embankment and play "train in the station." It was so exciting, standing on the platform pretending a train was coming, running back and forth on the tracks screeching "choo-choo."

I wanted so much to see that first train approach the station at the new bridge. But I never saw that train. And I never saw the finished bridge.

* * * * *

3

My Childhood Village

If SPEYER HAD BEEN my only childhood home, it alone would have given me enough rich experiences for a lifelong wellspring of memories. As I began to lift those memories, buried for nearly half a century, rich remembrances began to surface about the village of Schwegenheim, where I had spent my earliest years.

There were no pictures of Schwegenheim on my walls. It wasn't as picturesque as Speyer, it had no Altpörtel, no famous churches, no Rhine. But in its own way it was just as flavorful. The village had even more dirt streets, farms, and woods. *And Schwegenheim had an unforgettable train.*

* * * * *

My mother and her whole family were raised in Schwegenheim. Their ancestors went back for generations in and around the village. My grandfather, my *Opa*, Ludwig Walther, was born in Schwegenheim. People called him Loui. My grandmother, *Oma*, Carolina—Lina for short—was born in the nearby village of Gommersheim. Opa ran a small general store in their house on Bahnhofstrasse (Railroad Street), and he was also a butcher.

Faded snapshots show the house as a one-story cement structure with a dormer-like attic. Opa's store was at one end. A photo shows my mother standing on the single step at the entrance, flanked by display windows, in one window some cans and boxes that look like groceries, in the other some dark-colored cloth objects hanging on stands. Since my mother was a milliner, I suppose these are the hats she displayed in the store.

My mother started her career at fifteen as an apprentice in a large millinery factory in the city of Karlsruhe on the edge of the beautiful Schwarzwald, the Black Forest. Whenever she referred to Karlsruhe, she did so with nostalgia. I got the impression that Karlsruhe was like another world to my provincial mother. In those days, it was hours on the train from Schwegenheim, although today it is about an hour's drive.

When she was in her early twenties, Mother returned to Schwegenheim and began to make ladies' hats. She went by bicycle to other villages to take orders from customers, and delivered them the same way. Apparently her business flourished even during poor times after World War I, since wearing hats was obligatory for various occasions. By the midtwenties, she had built up a steady business. Aunt Selma, who was by then in her late teens and who had also trained in Karlsruhe, worked with her.

In 1925, when my mother was thirty-one, she married Otto Stern, who lived in the big city of Mannheim about twenty-five miles north of Schwegenheim. When they settled in a house on Bahnhofstrasse near my grandparents, they became the tenth Jewish family among about three hundred families in the village.

I have no memories of my first house in Schwegenheim, since we moved out when I was very small. The old photos show that it was right next to my grandparents', separated by a walled-in yard. Since it was on a corner of an intersecting street, my family referred to it as the *Eckhaus*. Reviewing those old photos now, I became aware for the first time that the *Eckhaus* was once my home.

My father worked in a chemical factory as a young man. He used to tell me about that with a mixture of pride, and nostalgia. "I worked in the laboratory," he would say. "We made

Sauerstoff. You know what that is?" And I would always answer, "Oxygen." Then he'd exhort me to become a chemist, or a glassblower. "Glassblowers make good money making laboratory equipment. Having a trade is the best thing!" I always hated those lectures. And one day as I was thinking about visiting his native city of Mannheim, I realized that although I had never been especially proud of him and often resented him, I was now beginning to try to understand him better.

I discovered that the chemical factory was in Ludwigshafen, the industrial city across the river from Mannheim—not in Speyer as I had assumed all these years. In the 1920s, a trip from Schwegenheim to Ludwigshafen must have been a long one. He would have to take a train from Schwegenheim to Speyer, then another to Ludwigshafen.

I imagined that in the wee hours of the morning, my father would walk the short distance from our house to the station, sometimes in mud because Bahnhofstrasse was a dirt street. He would board a little train, the narrow gauge railroad that connected the villages with Speyer, where he'd board a big train. In the evening, he took the same long trip back. Perhaps, I imagined, he sometimes stayed overnight in Mannheim with his relatives.

The little train that connected the villages with Speyer was something special for everyone in the area. No, it was more than special. It was treasured—a dear little train that got into your bones and your very soul. Even its name brought loving smiles to people's cheeks: *Der Pfefferminzzug,* the Peppermint Train.

Peppermint was a major crop of Schwegenheim and neighboring villages, and the farmers shipped their harvest on that little train, to Speyer, and to Neustadt on the other end of the line. It ran a mere twenty-mile stretch, and the villages it served had names that sounded to me as endearing as the train itself: Dudenhofen-Harthausen-Schwegenheim-Weingarten-Freisbach-Gommersheim-Geinsheim-Duttenweiler-Lachen.

The villagers and townsfolk used affectionate diminutives when referring to their *Pfefferminzzug,* such as *Pfefferminzzügel* or *Pfefferminzzügele* and *Pfefferminzbähnel,* in translation, all variations on the "little Peppermint Train." But no

The Peppermint Train 17

English translation can recreate the childlike pleasure evoked by the sound of those German diminutives. And the words still evoke in me the aroma and taste of the peppermint tea we drank so often.

Men went to work on the *Pfefferminzzügele*. Women rode it on one of its four daily runs to shop in the large stores and markets in Speyer and Neustadt. I imagine that Mother would ride the train to visit customers in bad weather or if they lived too far for her to go by bicycle.

In any case, the little *Pfefferminzzug* became part of my life from the day I was born. On the seventeenth of July in 1927, my pregnant mother took the little train to Speyer, entered the hospital, and brought me into the world two days later. Then on the twenty-ninth, she placed her Egon in a basket, walked to the train station, and took me for my first ride on the Peppermint Train.

When Mother arrived at the little station in Schwegenheim, carrying me in my basket, my grandmother was waiting for us. According to family legend, Oma took one look at us and said, "Give me that child." Then, my four-foot-eleven-inch spry-as-a-chicken grandmother hurried me to her house on Bahnhofstrasse.

For some time after that, my Oma and Opa raised me while my parents remained in the background. To this day I wonder if my pint-sized grandmother was possessive or if my mother didn't know what to do with me. I'd even had thoughts that Mother abandoned me. But ultimately I reached a less subjective conclusion: Like many other children, I was cared for by grandparents while my parents made a living.

My mother, thirty-three when I was born, was an active businesswoman. Only an inch taller than her mother, she was even more ambitious and able-bodied. She never sat still. I even heard that as soon as she got home from the hospital, she started making the rounds again on her bicycle and went with my Aunt Selma to millinery exhibitions in distant cities. My father worked long hours at the chemical factory while at the same time planning to open a millinery store in Speyer. He was in some ways the opposite of my mother, more sedate, not at all prone to histrionics, but he too was ambitious. He was a bookkeeper, had impeccable handwriting and a machine-like speed with numbers. I remembered those two facts well, because he drilled into me the importance of good handwriting and fast arithmetic. Even after I left home, as an adult, he criticized one of my letters: "What kind of handwriting is that!"

While my parents worked, I certainly didn't lack attention. There was Oma and Opa, and Aunt Selma, and Mother's brother, Uncle Leon, who used to tease me and tweak my nose and pull my ears. And as I studied the old photos I began to see that there were plenty of neighbors who played with me, too. They are shown with Egon in the baby carriage, with his shock of curly blond hair and winsome, squinch-eyed smile.

Some of those snapshots show a young girl at my baby carriage. She was Mariele. Her name continued to crop up in family conversations long after we came to America. I'd heard that my grandfather was especially fond of her and showered her with gifts. One photo shows her as the bridesmaid at Aunt Selma's wedding. As I looked at that photo, I tried to remember more about Mariele, but she was just a name to me rather than someone who, I'd heard, was like "part of our family." My curiosity about her began to build.

When my parents moved to Speyer after opening their store there, I stayed with Oma and Opa. If I missed my mother and father, there was one glorious aspect to living apart from them: I got to ride the Peppermint Train whenever I was taken to visit them. Even after I joined them I often shuttled back and forth. Every time one of my nursemaids quit or was fired, back to Schwegenheim I went. I remember a summer day in front of our Speyer house when I was about four or five and my father said, "What are we going to do with him? He can't go to school yet, and he can't stay home by himself." So back to Schwegenheim I went.

With all that shuttling back and forth, Egon and the Peppermint Train became good friends. But soon the shuttling stopped. My grandfather had had another accident. One leg already crippled, a cow fell on his other leg. A cow? That's the way I understood the story, though often I wondered how a cow could fall on somebody. In any case, he walked with even more difficulty now. Besides, he and my grandmother were already in their sixties, and I needed someone to take care of me. So they came to live with us in Speyer.

Although my little Peppermint Train was no longer the close companion that ferried me between two homes, I didn't lose my dear friend altogether. My train would sometimes meet me at the station in Speyer and take me and my family to visit relatives in Schwegenheim and my grandmother's relatives, the Loebs, in Gommersheim. My "uncle" Julius—he was really a cousin but I called all adult relatives "uncle" or "aunt"—was a tall stocky man. He had a big family (since I had no brothers or sisters, anybody who had more than two children was a big family). The Loebs lived in a big stone house on the main street of Gommersheim.

So the Peppermint Train continued as a source of pleasure during those visits to my uncles, aunts, and cousins. And my fondness for that little train grew and grew.

* * * * *

I had yet another childhood romance in the little village of Schwegenheim. I loved its woods. Throughout my life those Schwegenheim woods remained as much a beacon of my German boyhood as the train. Even many of my dreams were about woods.

During the spring of 1983, the beloved woods of Schwegenheim came to mind again, and I imagined walking down Bahnhofstrasse, past the train station, and onto the friendly forest path to say a silent hello to the cordial trees. "If I should get to those woods," I said to Milly, "you may see me cry." I knew already that I'd have to spend some time in them alone.

I recalled that Oma and Aunt Selma, and my mother too sometimes, would put me in a big wooden cart, or wheelbarrow, roll it into the woods, and then scamper off into the underbrush between the tall trees. They'd bend over and like pecking chickens would pick up *Hutzele* and put them in their aprons and their sacks.

Milly asked, "What are hootsele?"

"Not hootsele," I replied. "Like in *put: Hutzele.*" I wasn't sure anymore exactly what they were. I only knew they used them for the fire in the stove at home.

One trip into those woods had stayed in my mind with great clarity, even though I must have been very young, maybe three. Oma, Aunt Selma, and mother were rolling me along the path in the wooden cart and they stopped at a small clearing. They spread some kind of cloth on the ground, probably a blanket, sat me down and put a basketful of grapes in front of me. Then they ran off into the woods gleefully cackling like chickens and picked *Hutzele* from the ground. I glowed as I pulled off and munched those sweet tiny yellow grapes in the warm sunny clearing between the towering trees. I only heard the laughter of the women, the birds, the rustle of leaves. No one else was there. I think I felt that the woods were ours—in fact, that they were mine.

They returned, gay and excited, and emptied their collections into the wagon. Suddenly, there was a distant thunderclap. "*Schnell, schnell,*" my mother exclaimed, scooping me up into the wagon, too. Rolling homeward amidst the *Hutzele*, I saw a fiery arrow up in the sky, then another, and soon was witnessing a fire-fight up in heaven. Thunderclaps came closer. I felt drops of wetness on my face.

* * * * *

It was shortly after those reminiscences about the Schwegenheim woods that I had the terrifying nightmare about "the man who could do everything and stopped at nothing" destroying my salamander and my trees—that man who, in the woods of Germany and other lands, destroyed all those millions of innocent people.

And despite the warm feelings I had for the woods and the train, I wondered how I could go back to them. Then, in the depth of despair, almost ready to cancel the trip, I realized that I could not hate the woods of Schwegenheim. They did no one any harm. Their trees were innocent, and were always my loyal friends. And I could not be angry with my childhood companion, the Peppermint Train.

The train, the trees, the *Hutzele*, the Bahnhofstrasse, sometimes dusty, sometimes muddy, formed my first impressions of the world, a simple warm world. For Egon, there was no such thing as television, not even a radio in the early days of Schwegenheim; there was no family car, not even a horse and carriage. Little Egon lived in a world of a stone house with a wood stove and chicken and geese in the yard. However painful it might be, I needed to go back to see if even a fragment of that warm, simple boyhood world still stood.

*   *   *   *   *

4

"Juden Verboten"

Speyer, Schwegenheim, and Gommersheim formed the provincial orbit of my boyhood. It was an orbit of a mere ten miles.

On special occasions, I stepped out of that little orbit to visit relatives in places that were to me like distant satellites. In the faraway villages of Dolgesheim and Seeheim, I did exciting things I couldn't do in my own hometowns. In Dolgesheim I got to ride with an "uncle" in his horse and buggy. In Seeheim there was a big swimming pool.

The two big cities I visited were like different worlds: cities to which I would travel on big trains that made exciting loud sounds, cities in which I saw bustling people, trolley cars, huge ornate fountains in spacious green parks, and buildings where people lived high up, buildings that were taller than anything in Speyer, even taller than the Altpörtel. One of these cities was Kaiserslautern, where Aunt Selma had moved after she married Uncle Eugene. The other was Mannheim, where my father's relatives lived.

My father's mother came to Germany from Czechoslovakia as a child. When she married, she settled in Mannheim and had nine children, of whom six sons and one daughter survived infancy. Although I was not as close to my father's family as I was to my mother's, I knew all of them except one, Richard, who died in World War I fighting for Germany. The youngest, Arthur, was killed by the Germans in the Holocaust.

Pondering this irony as I turned to their photos in my father's archives, I came across an antique photo-postcard of my Uncle Willie in his World War I uniform. He looked like a prototypical German soldier: erect posture in knee-high boots, one leg jutting forward, left arm crooked with the hand clutching the buckle of a big belt around a hip-length brass buttoned jacket, a tassel hanging from his side. To me, his face looked as Aryan as any—slanted eyes, straight nose, and thin mouth—and to top it all off, on his head sat one of those ornate spiked Kaiser helmets. In reality, Uncle Willie was anything but militaristic. I remembered him as warm and kind. Yet, he'd posed proudly in that German uniform. In World War II, the only uniform he wore was the striped one of the concentration camp.

Another brother, Ino, is shown in a World War I uniform with a long saber at his waist. Ino never got to a concentration camp. He was killed during an Allied bombing raid on Mannheim.

And the irony crossed my mind that soon after Uncle Willie came home from the concentration camp, his daughter Lore married a gentile German. "Well, whatever Lore's husband did during the war," I said to Milly, "he did marry a person of Jewish extraction. That says something about him. It'll be interesting to see what he's like."

I also seemed to remember that after the war Uncle Willie even worked in a Jewish cemetery—probably the one in Mannheim.

I turned to the photo of the large black marble memorial on my father's mother's grave in Mannheim. She had died in 1937, but after the war the family erected a new memorial to include the names of their relatives who died in the concentration camps. I exclaimed, "My God! If Uncle Willie did work in that cemetery, how must he have felt whenever he walked by that grave?"

"It's a crazy world," Milly sighed.

Tense from the conversation, I started to jabber. "What some of my relatives went through! It makes my story trivial by comparison. As a matter of fact, these last couple of weeks the words 'I was thrown out' keep coming to me. That I was thrown out of Germany. I'd never thought of it like that before. I always considered myself an emigrant, émigré . . . is there a difference? In any case we left on our own accord. But I felt thrown out, kicked out. Even when I was talking to somebody last week about my plans to go back, I used the words 'I was kicked out.' And they said, 'Really, Ed?' It started me thinking."

Milly interrupted me. "What did you mean by your story being trivial by comparison?"

The question annoyed me. My emotions were already at a boil, and she hadn't understood my point. "Can't you see! Here I am, feeling guilty, really guilty, about merely being 'thrown out!' While others were tortured, shot, burned; a few lucky ones survived the horrors of the camps. I just don't understand it, just can't figure it out. What good did our religion do? Where was God?"

"Lots of people have been trying to understand that for a long time," Milly said.

I sat silently, thinking. Later that night, I came to realize that an important reason for my going back lay in something Milly said: "trying to understand." Sure, I was going back for nostalgia, for the fond memories. But I needed to try to understand, to learn something, maybe to reconcile something.

Mannheim came back to mind, and I wondered if I'd get to see it. Maybe I'd even take a train ride, on a big German train, from Speyer to Ludwigshafen, then the trolley to Mannheim, like Egon used to do with his father. Though there would be no exciting steam engine as in Egon's trips, Edgar could get on the train, close his eyes, and imagine.

That big train, twice the size of the Peppermint Train, would roll into the grand Ludwigshafen station, amidst toots, whistles, screeches of brakes on huge iron wheels, hissing puffs of steam, people reaching up to racks above their heads to get their luggage, in an instant followed by metallic clangs as feet pounded on iron steps and descended to the concrete platform below. Then I'd walk swiftly beside my father, past more steam, toots, whistles, huge clocks, conductors shouting, loudspeakers announcing, finally entering a waiting hall so immensely spacious, and its ceiling so high up that I thought it must be touching heaven, maybe even God.

Voices blared from gray cones high up on the walls, big blackboards showed rows of white letters and numbers, little two-wheeled and four-wheeled carts with nervously bouncing suitcases and boxes were urgently being rolled by men with colorful caps on their heads; people stood, people walked, people sat on long wooden benches that looked something like the benches in our synagogue. The clamorous hurry-scurry at the same time stimulated and dulled my senses, till my father led me through gigantic glass doors to the sidewalk outside.

There on the street would be brightly colored, slender, oval-ended trolley cars, some cozily hitched together in pairs, some even in triplets, their optimistic clanging bells beckoning invitingly to my ears. We would clamber aboard our car, I would sit tightly but expectantly, ears tuned to sounds and eyes glued to sights that I could never hear and see in quiet little Speyer: wide streets with tracks, the honking of many cars, buildings that grew into the sky, a conductor punching holes into the ticket my father was holding. The trolley would then pass under an ornate arch onto a bridge. As we moved across the bridge, I would watch the water flicker behind the latticed girders and, in the distance, smoke from spiraling chimneys reaching higher to God than even the tall buildings. Then the trolley would slow, the conductor would call "Mannheim," and my toes would start to get up; but we stayed on. While I hypnotically watched the flow of trolley tracks and the passing parade of big buildings, the conductor came to punch another hole in my father's ticket. Then I'd marvel at a park with gaily spouting fountains, another with statues of horses, another with statues of men, and soon I saw buildings with curtained windows, some of them open, some with blankets and comforters hanging out, sometimes a woman shaking a rug.

When we got off the trolley we would walk a short distance to a street where my grandmother lived in one of those buildings, a street without a name, only a letter and a number: "S-2." We then climbed endless steps that made me pant, to the very top floor where my grandmother greeted us.

That is how I remembered Mannheim.

My father's mother was much taller and thinner than my other grandmother, slower moving, and not as warm. She was a more remote grandmother whom I don't even remember calling *"Oma."*

My other grandfather I never even met. Long before I was born, he deserted his family, an event that my father often alluded to when he lectured me to be grateful for what he provided me. He would refer resentfully to having had to live in a *"Waisenhaus"* when he was a boy, which, though for many years I didn't understand, was an orphanage. But my father always respected his mother. And he always remained fond of his native Mannheim. So did I, always feeling sort of a warm glow whenever I heard the name connected with anything, like "the *Mannheim* school of music" and the town of Manheim that I often passed through in Pennsylvania.

One day when I was studying a map of Germany with Milly, it struck me how many German towns and cities end with "heim." I felt a warm connection. Maybe they reminded me of my own Schwegenheim, Gommersheim, and Mannheim. Suddenly I jerked my head up from the map and grabbed the German dictionary. Yes, *Heim* is the German word for "home." I had never been conscious of it before. *Heim* reminds me of home when I was little. *Heimat*, a homeland where I wasn't wanted any more, where I was kicked out. Even before I was born, Hitler vowed in *Mein Kampf* that the Jews had to get out of Germany. But lots of them didn't believe it.

My father did. If he hadn't gotten out and I'd have survived the hell, I wonder if I'd still have any warm feelings for that *Heimat.*

I found myself getting angry at Germany again. But the warm feelings stayed too, along with sadness. The feelings went back and forth: when I felt the sadness, there was usually a layer of warmth underneath, and when I felt the warmth, there was a layer of sadness, and increasingly over these weeks, anger. It was these feelings fighting with each other that made my memories appear and disappear, like constantly alternating weather—from sun and warmth, to cloud and chill, and back again. As we got closer to the trip, my weather turned cloudy more of the time. Once it was so dark I remarked to Milly that I didn't want to see any of those places at all. But that feeling didn't last long.

I searched the map for Kaiserslautern, reminding Milly that Aunt Selma had her millinery store there. Uncle Eugene worked with furs in the back. I vaguely recalled that it was on a busy street, and I remembered seeing trolleys nearby. I clearly recalled their apartment too, in a big complex built in the round. I had spent many days there playing with my cousin Gerd.

My mind drifted back to Dolgesheim and Seeheim. Whenever I would visit Dolgesheim, I told Milly, Uncle Moses would pick us up at a little railroad station in his horse and buggy. We'd go up a long steep hill to their house, and, on the way back, going down, the buggy would go so fast that I'd worry about what would happen if the horse couldn't run anymore and the buggy kept on going.

Seeheim was the home of "Uncle" Hugo and "Aunt" Lillian, Oma's sister's daughter. Once Aunt Lillian and my mother took me to a big public swimming pool there. I must have been about eight. A sign at the entrance read *Juden Verboten*—Jews Not Allowed. Aunt Lillian must have thought it safe to go in anyhow.

* * * * *
5

What Did Egon Do Wrong?

BY THE TIME I was born, Hitler had made a name for himself and many had joined his Nazi party. In mass rallies he threatened not only the Jews but the whole world. "The time will come," he ranted in Nuremberg, "when those responsible for Germany's collapse will laugh out of the other side of their faces. Fear will grip them. Let them know that their judgment day is on the way."

Hitler's pronouncements began to pervade even the small villages and towns across the land, including the places where I lived and visited. But all I knew was the world of the baby carriage in my grandparents' garden, the *Eckhaus*, my parents, Oma and Opa, loving uncles, aunts, and cousins, my synagogue and my family's Jewish rituals and holiday celebrations, the neighbors who played with me, the wheelbarrow rides and the *Hutzele* in the woods, the Peppermint Train. I wasn't aware of the huge Nazi parades and fanfare in the big cities, and I wasn't aware that Hitler's ideas were beginning to poison the minds of some of my neighbors.

Most adults weren't aware, either, that Hitler's threats and the Nazi movement would bring tragedy. Even as 200,000 Nazis marched in Nuremberg, I and my family and Christian neighbors continued to live peacefully with each other.

Egon didn't know that there were Nazi organizations in Speyer, even before he moved there, and that some people had started to avoid his parents and grandparents because they were Jewish. Egon didn't know that Hitler even denounced Jewish children and that "all Jews" were to blame, including little Egon himself. Egon was a happy little three-year-old in idyllic surroundings even as six and a half million Germans voted for the Nazi party, whose storm troopers in Berlin sang:

The Storm Troops stand at ready
The racial fight to lead.
Until the Jews are bleeding
We know we are not freed.

At the age of five Egon couldn't comprehend that his country's democracy was crumbling. Even then, in 1932 and 1933, many Jews and non-Jews alike still believed the Nazis would disappear, that they were just a temporary craze. To be sure, many Jews were getting very anxious. Some even started to leave the country. But Egon's good life went on: he rode the little trains and big trains to the villages and cities where his adoring relatives lived. He went with his Opa to the Messplatz in Speyer and gathered chestnuts. And his family's business continued to thrive.

But soon things began to happen close to home, and Egon gradually became exposed to his parents' anxieties. One day he had a scary experience while accompanying his father and mother to a Speyer school building. As they approached the school, he saw people milling around, some in brown uniforms, some with swastikas on their arms. The big heavy wooden entrance door was open, and adults were going in and out. Inside, he also saw men with brown uniforms, and swastikas. Egon became afraid. His parents seemed unusually tense, he thought, their faces tightly set. They looked straight ahead in taut silence and Egon felt his mother's hand tighten on his as they went inside and up the marble steps. They walked briskly down the hall and into a large room, where more men and women stood. Egon saw two huge boxes with slits on top. They looked like immense toy coin-banks. On tables lay big heavy notebooks, like the ones in his father's office in the store. Egon's father and mother went to one of those tables, said their names, and wrote something in the book. The woman at the table handed each of them a slip of white paper. Egon noticed some printing on it but couldn't read it.

There were booths in the room with curtains in front, like Egon once saw in the hospital when his mother took him for an examination. But in this schoolroom there were no doctors, and inside each booth was a small stand with pencils on it. Egon stood with his father and watched his mother go into a booth, close the curtain, and quickly come out again with her paper now folded. She slid it into one of the boxes. Then he stood holding his mother's hand while his father quickly did the same thing. Egon's parents hadn't said a word to each other since they had arrived at the school. Their faces stayed tight as they hastened toward the stairs, looking neither left nor right at the people who stood there. But Egon, with his head lowered, peeked out of the corner of his eye and noticed some of the people watching him and his parents. A couple of them had smirks on their faces and one seemed to be glowering at them. For sure, Egon thought, they were being watched because they were Jewish. He'd overheard his parents' worried conversation earlier that morning about the dangers of going to vote against Hitler, but that they wouldn't bother anyone who had a child along. At that thought, Egon looked up straight into the face of one of the men, just as he felt the tug of his mother's hand as they rushed down the stairs and out onto the sidewalk.

They walked rapidly away from the school, stopped, and looked in the direction of the store, then toward home. There were anxious whispers, and Egon heard his father say, "Take him home, I'll go back to the store."

Not long after that, Hitler became head of Germany. Then one day anti-Jewish posters were pasted on his parents' store windows, and another day uniformed men stood in front telling people not to enter and not to buy from Jews. Egon was at home with his Oma and Opa that Saturday in April 1933, and he didn't realize what it meant that all Jewish businesses were being boycotted.

That year, Jews left Germany in great numbers, but many others thought things would get better again. Even many Christians had complained about the boycott and the Nazis eased up. Egon's family's business continued to do well.

Meanwhile, Egon was beginning to grow up; his connection with his German surroundings deepened. He was becoming more attached to the sights, sounds, and smells of his native city. He rode the trolleys in Mannheim, hiked with his family in the woods of Kaiserslautern, thrilled at the horse and buggy rides in Dolgesheim, played on the new railroad embankment, went on a train across the pontoon bridge, and rode the Peppermint Train.

Egon was enjoying all that even as the secret police began to bring terror into people's hearts and Göring, Hitler's right-hand man, warned that it was not his business to do justice but "to annihilate and exterminate."

Egon loved his surroundings even while signs went up in many places telling the Jews to get out, *"Juden raus,"* and even when a brown-shirted boy threatened to beat him up on his way to school. Egon was lucky that in those early Hitler days his parents could still ask the boy's family to make him stop.

Egon was never physically attacked, but there were other anxious moments. One day, all the schoolchildren were assembled in a movie theater to see a film about Adolph Hitler. When the assemblage stretched out their arms in the Hitler salute, Egon stiffened with fear as his Jewish classmates looked at each other and as their Jewish teacher signaled with his eyes and one student whispered, "Don't, we don't have to." After the movie they quickly rushed off to avoid the stares and insults of some of the other children.

As the Nazis got tougher, Egon began to hear his family talk about where they could go if they had to leave Germany. Some Jews considered nearby countries in Europe such as France and Switzerland, a few considered remote places like Argentina or South Africa, but most favored America or Palestine.

Egon's father was a Zionist. One warm day, Egon watched as his father sat at a small table outside the synagogue selling tickets for a movie about Palestine. When his father ran short of change, he asked Egon to go get some at the store. Egon ran quickly, nervous about not losing the bill for change and eager not to miss any part of the movie.

In that film Egon saw Palestine for the first time. People explained kibbutz life. Tanned boys and girls danced gaily and sang Hebrew songs. When the movie ended with *"Hatikva,"* the Jewish national anthem, Egon's skin tingled. But his family's talk about going to Palestine made him feel sad. He saw no woods in the movie like the ones in Schwegenheim and Speyer; everything looked different, even the houses; and the people spoke a language he couldn't understand.

Egon didn't want to go anyplace else. He liked it where he lived. But he also felt puzzled that some of his playmates stopped playing with him and that the family across from his school wouldn't let him leave his bicycle at their house anymore. Egon sometimes wondered what he had done that was wrong. He began to be afraid.

In 1935, the Nazis passed the Nuremberg laws that took more rights away from the Jews, and one of those laws affected Egon very personally. Not long after summer vacation, the principal came to his class and announced that Jewish children were no longer allowed in the school. A few days later, Egon and the other Jewish children started going to the synagogue for all their studies.

Egon's parents lost many customers, and his father insisted that the Nazis would only get worse. The family had to decide where to go. His father had written to relatives in America. One of Oma's two sisters had emigrated to America in the 1800s, and she had two daughters, Ruby and Amelia. Amelia had married Samuel Schloss, a wealthy man in Montgomery, Alabama. They were "millionaires," my mother used to say. Their wholesale grocery business was known throughout the South. Would they help us come to America? The Schlosses wrote back that it would be better to go to Palestine, but the family questioned whether they could earn a living there. "It's too hot there for hats and furs, and we can't make a living on yarmulkes," Uncle Eugene joked. But he agreed we had to leave— the Nazis in Kaiserslautern were even worse than in Speyer.

The Peppermint Train   33

But Palestine? That pioneering country wasn't the place for Egon's grandparents either, assuming that the family could send for them later. Especially for his crippled Opa. Also, Opa reminded the family that he had visited America when he was young and had liked it there.

By now, all of Egon's relatives were talking about leaving, and nobody would go to Palestine if they could help it. Egon's father wrote again to the Schlosses, explaining how bad things were getting and assuring them that the family could take care of themselves in America. All they needed was to have the sponsorship papers signed.

Egon's father sent him to take English lessons.

* * * * *
6

My Chocolate Farewell

EVERY YEAR BEFORE Hanukkah, our Hebrew School teacher, *Lehrer* Marx, who was also our rabbi, would ask each of us what we wanted for a gift. Then he'd make us a big party. In my first year of Hebrew school, when I was six, the students howled with laughter when I announced that I wanted nothing but *"Eine Torte,"* a chocolate layer cake. Suppressing his own laughter, Mr. Marx thought for a moment and chuckled, "Well, Egon, I will see what I can do about a torte."

My announcement got back to my family. How my face flushed with embarrassment when my father, with a serious mien, questioned, "How did you come to choose a chocolate cake?"

At the party, everybody else had received their gifts and my head had almost disappeared into my shoulders as I wondered about *my* gift, when suddenly Mr. Marx looked at me with a grin, spread his arms and blared "and now. . . ." My head popped up, the schoolroom door opened, and the teacher's wife walked in with a shiny round chocolate cake in her hands, as Mr. Marx chanted, *"Eine Torte für Egon."* Everyone giggled and clapped as our teacher laughed, "Baked by the best baker in Germany, Mrs. Marx."

Two years later, in 1935, when Rabbi Marx asked us what we wanted for Hanukkah, his voice and words reflected the times: "Even though we are sadder this year . . . and miss those who have already left us for distant lands . . . we will celebrate . . . and try our best to grant your wishes."

* * * * *

Some weeks after that 1935 Hanukkah party, my parents and I were on a night train. I had a slight cough from the tail end of a cold. My mother looked anxious throughout the long trip. Whenever I coughed she bent her small frame toward me whispering "Shsh, sh, don't cough." She was worried that the doctors at the American consulate in Stuttgart, where we were going, would think I had a disease and deny our visas to come to America.

* * * * *

On a warm Saturday in mid-June of 1936, two weeks before we were to leave for America, I took an unusual ride on the Peppermint Train.

My parents wanted to pay a farewell visit to the Loebs, our beloved relatives in Gommersheim. They had made arrangements for me to go by myself, and they would join me the next day. It was my first time on the train alone, and I was afraid.

I often wondered why my ordinarily meticulous father and anxious mother sent me on that train alone in those frightening times. They must have had good reasons—maybe some important business and emigration matters to take care of for which a child shouldn't be around. Maybe they reasoned that it was safe on a Saturday morning when few people rode the train to the villages. Besides, I didn't look Jewish.

They reassured me. I had ridden that train countless times. I should just make sure to wait three stops past Schwegenheim and walk to the Loebs' house as we'd done before. My parents would be there in the morning with Uncle Oscar, my father's brother from Mannheim. He would bring us all back in his car, which would be fun. But I didn't see fun written on their faces, and I worried. What would I do if somebody asked me if I was Jewish. Say *"nein,"* like Opa told me? But. . . .

Once I saw my little train at the station, I felt easier, and was eager to climb on right away. Oma gave me my ticket, explaining again that I should stay in my seat, be quiet, keep my head inside the window, and remember not to get off at Schwegenheim but wait for Gommersheim and go right to the Loebs' house. Then she handed me a big chocolate bar with a bright yellow wrapping and a ribbon, reminding me that it was my gift to the Loebs and I shouldn't eat it.

There I was by myself in the car. It was quiet. The locomotive hadn't started its engine yet. I sat tensely. I repeated to myself the names of the stations and fantasized what I'd do if I got off at the wrong one: Run after the train? Cry? Politely approach a kind-looking person? But even a kind-looking person might ask me if I'm Jewish.

My hand tightened on my gift chocolate bar. The early summer sun streamed through the windows. I started to feel hot. I looked at a shady spot, but remembered, "Stay in your seat." But no one else was in the car, so I moved, just in the nick of time because then two screaming children raced up the steps into my coach, a woman behind them.

I tensed, glanced at them and quickly looked down at my chocolate bar. I didn't move. Nothing happened. The woman opened windows and I felt cooler. When I looked up, we nodded to each other. She didn't see that I'm Jewish, I thought, or it didn't matter to her.

There was a distant train whistle, and soon a big train rumbled into the main station. As I watched people get off and people get on, I felt the familiar jolt of my Peppermint Train. Its engine took its first breath. A few people who had left the big train came towards us. I again became afraid. I saw two men approach. They had loud voices and were wearing big boots. The sound of their boots pounded on my ears as they stepped aboard. My eyes turned down at my chocolate bar. Their voices softened, and I caught sight of their smiles and heard them say, *"Guten Tag. Es wird heiss heute."* They're right, I thought, it will be hot today.

As the big train left the station, the Peppermint Train blew its whistle, and we began to move. A breeze cooled my perspiring face, and I carefully held my softening chocolate bar upright so it would also cool.

As my *Pfefferminzzug* headed toward its first stop, I felt better. No one had bothered me. As I took in the familiar fragrances and sights of fields, farms, and woods and watched the smoke billow from the chugging locomotive, I settled into cozy contentment with the rocking, meandering motion of the train.

Today, I wonder to what extent nine-year-old Egon realized that drastic changes were to take place in his life and to what extent he sensed the emotional ordeal his family was going through. Yes, he had been taking English lessons, he had taken a worrisome trip to Stuttgart, and he "knew" he was going to America. He must have felt sad, if not depressed, about leaving his grandparents, even just from seeing them looking so sad.

But on that last trip to Gommersheim, America was just the name of a faraway place—more than a week on a boat, they had told me. Like any child, I was concerned with more immediate things: my gift of chocolate for the Loebs, my sadness about leaving my woods and my Peppermint Train. I wonder now if perhaps it was really not my family who told me to go alone on the train that day; perhaps it was I who begged them to let me ride my train one last time, alone—despite my fears.

When I arrived in Gommersheim, the midday sun beat down on me and my chocolate bar. The streets were almost deserted, and when I approached the familiar whitewashed concrete wall fronting the courtyard of my relatives' house, I saw the shutters all tightly closed. I pushed open the wooden gate and walked to the door, but didn't hear a sound. Maybe they went away? No, I was told they knew I was coming. They're taking their midday nap.

I tapped lightly on the door, afraid of waking them. They didn't answer, so I walked down the street to the edge of the village where the open fields were, gingerly holding my softening gift. I walked into the field, amid grasses and grain taller than myself, breathing in the wonderful fragrances. I felt sad. My parents had told me we were going to live in a big city, the biggest in the world.

My chocolate bar was getting softer and softer. Maybe I should rush back to the house. But as I made my way toward the road, the package began to droop. I might as well eat it. If I didn't eat it it would just waste away.

As I began to peel the yellow wrapper, the inner foil oozed syrupy sauce. I feared getting it on my clothes and, holding it away from my body, bent low to put my tongue on it. Before I could take a second lick it slid from my trembling, sticky fingers onto the ground. I felt the taste of chocolate in my choked-up throat, and, looking down, I sadly envisioned marching ants. A fly landed on my cheek, and I walked away, lingering amidst the rows of grain. Thirsty and hungry, I returned to the Loeb house.

I knocked harder this time. When the door opened, Uncle Julius stood there adjusting his suspenders, grinning down at me with his gentle eyes, big ears, and little mustache. His pleasant round belly reached toward me as he said in his deep kind voice, "So, where were you? We were waiting for you." I started to stammer, "I was here before," when female voices inside the house chorused, *"Er ist da, Egon ist hier."*

Two weeks later, my German boyhood began to melt into oblivion.

* * * * *

7

Edgar

FATHER HAD ALREADY said good-bye and was waiting outside. Mother, still weeping bitterly, started down the stairs, then ran back up, then down again, several times, pulling her hair, wailing, "This is the end, we will never see each other again." Opa tried with his canes to negotiate the steep stairs, weeping that his life was over, he would kill himself.

We were in the tiny third-floor apartment in town, to which Oma and Opa had moved a few days before because they couldn't stay by themselves in our rural home on the outskirts of Speyer. Oma, besides herself, embracing and reembracing Mother and me, screamed at Opa to stop talking that way and to stay put lest he fall down the steps. Holding back tears, I felt the blood rushing through my head. Father came back in, saying, "Everything will be all right," trying to calm everyone. "We will send for you," he said to my grandparents; but I sensed he wasn't really sure. His own emotions seemed hidden behind the deep flush of his face as he took my mother and me by the hand and pulled us outside, saying, "We must hurry, there is a train to catch."

Uncle Oscar was waiting in his car to drive us to some distant railroad station to catch a train to Hamburg. There, a big boat waited to take us to America. It was June 29, 1936. The sun warmed my face. But at the sight of Uncle Oscar's boxlike black car, I suddenly felt cold, frightened, and my feet moved as if they bore lead weights. My shoulders drooped, my neck barely seemed to hold my head up.

Oma came rushing out of the house, tears streaming down her face. She leaned in for a final embrace. "Write soon," she wailed. The car pulled away, my throat choked back tears, I bit my lips.

In our last photos, in front of the house, Mother and Oma are holding handkerchiefs, as if they'd been crying, their dark dresses reinforcing their funereal look, and even my father looked sad. My winsome smile was gone.

The train ride to Hamburg was the longest I had ever taken. Though I slept in a berth and ate in a dining car, it was no fun. Mother alternated between silent tearfulness and frightened whispers. She feared we would be turned back before the boat left the German shore. Father seemed sadder than I'd ever seen him.

We met Aunt Selma, Uncle Eugene, and their son Gerd in Hamburg. Aunt Selma's jovial nature eased our somber mood. Even Mother perked up when Aunt Selma jingled her pocketbook full of German coins and led us to one ice-cream and candy store after another to spend it all. I never tasted so many different flavors of ice cream and I feasted on marzipan and other candies. Mother worried that I'd get sick, and we'd be turned back by the authorities. But I was having fun again.

That night in the hotel, my father reminded me to always wear my shoes till we got to America. Afterward, I found out why. He had put gold coins in my heels.

I had been told that we would travel on a big boat called the *Manhattan*, but when I saw it the next morning it was larger than I'd ever imagined a boat could be: huge gangplanks, big mouthlike openings into which things were being loaded, including immense wooden crates called lifts. I wondered which one of those lifts was ours, with all our furniture.

Mother's worrying subsided once the ship got under way. But soon she got seasick. She vomited a lot and stayed in our tiny cabin much of the eight-day voyage. My father never got sick, and I threw up only twice—once over the stern of the ship while watching the swirling tracks of the ship's movement in the ocean.

There were lots of new and fascinating things to see on the boat—especially the American movies, featuring Charlie Chaplin and Shirley Temple. There were two showings daily, and I sat through all of them. I learned to play shuffleboard. I marveled at the swimming pool on the deck. I ran around gleefully with Gerd and other children, many of them also Jewish boys and girls going to live in America. There was an American girl who talked to me in English, then laughed and ran away when I didn't understand. In the afternoons at tea time, Gerd and I would run to a little window on deck, ring the bell, and shout "cake," a word we had quickly learned. We also quickly learned to say "more cake," and to understand "all gone."

On the Fourth of July I saw for the first time how American Independence Day was celebrated. I lit my first sparkler. Five days later, my parents woke me up at dawn. *"Komm, steh auf,"* my mother said in an excited whisper. *"Willst du nicht de Statu ov Libity sehen!"* Shortly I was on deck peering sleepy-eyed through an early morning mist at a statue of a lady with a torch.

July 9, 1936, became etched in my mind as a turning point in my life. On the pier were signs with Hebrew letters. I had never seen Hebrew signs in public before. Father said they were really Yiddish. I saw tears in Mother's eyes and sensed that she felt as I did—tearful with joy, that here we would be free from persecution.

We were met by Jeannette Loeb, a distant cousin of Julius Loeb of Gommersheim and of Amelia Schloss. She took all six of us in a taxi to an apartment on 103rd Street near Lexington Avenue. The street teemed with shrieking children splashing around gushing fire hydrants. I had never seen such a sight before. And I had never seen black people before. Down the block, elevated trains screeched by, and in the other direction railroad trains ran on a viaduct. I had never heard so much noise all at once before. And Mother was miserably sick from the heat. It had turned out to be the hottest day in New York's history.

Worse yet, the apartment had roaches and bedbugs and, since it was on the first floor, right off the sidewalk, Aunt Selma and Mother were so terrified that Uncle Eugene and Father took turns that night standing guard, Uncle Eugene with his razor-sharp furrier knife handy.

In the morning, Jeannette apologized profusely. She had rented a cheap apartment because she didn't know how much we could afford. She took us up to Washington Heights to stay with Uncle Julius's daughter. It was my first subway ride. There weren't enough beds, so I was sent to sleep with a family a few houses away. The boy there spoke only English. I cried. He tried to calm me by showing me how to chew gum. I only half understood him, and when I swallowed it he rolled his eyes, shook his head, and said I shouldn't have. I thought something would happen to my stomach. I became so inconsolable that in the middle of the night they went to tell my parents. Then I was allowed to sleep on the floor, next to Mother.

When our furniture arrived we moved into a nearby apartment on Fairview Avenue. It was also on the first floor, but the front door was inside a main entrance, and the neighborhood was nicer. Fairview Avenue was a very steep hill, with St. Nicholas Avenue at the top, Broadway at the bottom. Two houses down from ours another steep hill converged with Fairview Avenue. I'd never seen such steep city streets before.

Our apartment had a huge living room, with one window that looked into a narrow concrete yard separating our house from the next one up the hill. The dining room, which became my parents' bedroom, and the kitchen overlooked a big side yard that connected with the next house down. Two bedrooms in back, one of which became mine and Gerd's, looked out on a high wall that had been cut into the cliffs above us. On top of the wall we could see fences that enclosed the houses that towered above ours. Gerd and I soon discovered that the huge black wall, just a few feet from our window, was frightening in a thunderstorm. One night when our parents went out to talk to people about getting jobs, lightning flashed off the wall, and crashes of thunder rattled our windows. Gerd was terrified and started crying, but I was six years older and bravely tried to reassure him, till I too started to whimper. We went into the living room until our parents returned.

New York City was a far cry from Speyer and Schwegenheim, but it made me happy that there were woods across from our house, and it wasn't long before I took to exploring them and climbing up and down their steep cliffs. Fairview Avenue formed the edge of a bluff from which you could see miles into the distance. From our roof four flights up, the view was spectacular. We could see Fort Tyron Park nearby, the whole of the Inwood section of the city, then the Bronx and the distant hills to the north.

Ten days after we arrived was my ninth birthday, the one that was almost ignored. But with the nickel my father gave me I bought my first ice-cream cone in the candy store up on St. Nicholas Avenue.

In August, the relatives from Alabama came to visit us. We were all gathered in the living room, with Jeannette acting as interpreter. Since Aunt Amelia talked fairly slowly in her warm southern drawl, I understood some of what she said when she pointed out that "Egon" and "Gerd" sounded too German. It would be better for us to have American names.

First they went down a list of names for me and settled on "Edgar." "Do you like 'Edgar'?" Jeannette asked me in German. "It is as close as we can get to Egon." I swallowed and nodded. For Gerd they took his German middle name, Bernhard, and made it into Bernard. When my mother took me to register at P.S. 189—at 189th Street and Amsterdam Avenue—I was enrolled for the fourth grade as Edgar Egon Stern.

The first day of school my mother told me to wear my blue German sailor suit which had a big collar down the back and shorts. When I saw all the other boys wearing knickers, I felt odd. I cried when my mother started to leave, but my fourth grade teacher was kind and told her to stay till class started.

Most of the American children were friendly. Some made fun of my middle name Egon, a few called me a "refucheese." Soon "Egon" disappeared altogether, and I retained him only as a middle initial. It wasn't long before I'd get red in the face whenever someone called me Egon, even at home.

In October, another German-Jewish refugee joined the class.

She and I became champion spellers, and the teacher told everybody how amazing it was that two children who at first knew practically no English could make such fast progress. Within a year, everybody marveled that I'd completely lost my German accent. I beamed, proud of becoming an American boy.

Mother and Aunt Selma went to work cleaning other people's homes. I sometimes accompanied Mother to the "rich" people's huge apartments on West End Avenue, and during lunch breaks I would help her with her English lessons. Eventually she got a job in a dress factory and was much happier but ran into other problems, like getting sick from the cleaning fluids. Then one day she came home proudly laughing that she had been promoted to "inspector." She worked for a long time in the clothing industry and eventually wound up making hats again.

Father became an unskilled worker in a millinery factory. He didn't like it, but he worked hard. Uncle Eugene was luckier because he was a furrier, a trade in much demand.

In 1937, my grandparents came to America. What jubilation! Everybody went down to the pier. When I saw Oma walk down the gangplank, alone, my heart sank. I feared they'd left Opa behind. Then I saw him being brought out on deck in a wheel chair, and as they rolled him down the plank I ran up to him, weeping with joy.

With eight of us now crowded into the Fairview Avenue apartment, the going got rougher. My father and Uncle Eugene started arguing more; my mother and Aunt Selma alternately fought, didn't talk to each other, and made up; my grandparents got caught in the middle and started fighting with each other, Oma blaming my father, Opa siding with my parents, Mother being angry with Opa. I never understood what it was all about, and it made me very sad.

My parents moved down the hill to Broadway Terrace, a side street connecting Fairview Avenue with Broadway. Our apartment was three flights up on the top floor—my father didn't like people living on top of him. The scenery wasn't as nice as on Fairview Avenue—instead of woods there were rows of houses across the street—but it was only a minute's walk up the hill to the woods. Besides, I spent a lot of time on the roof, only a few steps from our apartment.

Friends of my parents got me a job as a delivery boy in a drycleaning store owned by German-Jewish people. They put a beret on my head with the name of the store on it, which made me feel embarrassed, and I didn't stay there long. My next job was in a bakery. I vividly remember struggling with two trunks full of bread and challahs that I delivered all over Washington Heights and Inwood. After that job I delivered groceries, and learned to hoist loads up to people's apartments on dumbwaiters from the basements. On the walls next to the dumbwaiters were dirty poems describing people who didn't tip enough. For two years I worked for the nervous man who out of the clear would shout: *"Ja hat er gesagt! Und dann ist er kaputt gegangen."*

I think my resentment of my father grew in those years. I remember being disappointed that he wasn't going to attend my grade school graduation. He didn't want to lose time from work, and besides, he told me, I didn't get any awards. Mother begged him to go, so he agreed. But he said congratulations only reluctantly. And he never attended any of my Boy Scout functions, not even when I was awarded an honor medal.

In 1943, my parents opened a small millinery store on 181st Street. Mother worked in the store six days a week and sometimes even went in on Sundays. Father kept the books and continued to work in the same factory where he'd started in 1936. He helped in the store evenings and Saturdays if it was busy and ran errands to the wholesalers downtown. He and Mother often quarreled about the business. That was something else I never really understood. I sided with Mother. In fact, I used to make fun of his being such a "stern" figure, and I resented his critical attitude toward me. When I told him I would like to become a teacher, he said, "What, you? A teacher. Learn a trade!" And when I asked him to sign a paper for permission to take an elective course in poetry, he ridiculed me, signing only after I'd begged him. In retrospect, considering the world's war and my own war with my father, it was probably no coincidence that I chose as my term project "Will Wars Ever End?"

In 1944, my parents, like thousands of other refugees that year, proudly became American citizens. Automatically, I was now a citizen too. But I wanted my very own documents. I guess I wanted the proof in my own possession that I was an American. I recall too, the pride I felt when I was ceremoniously sworn in, with dozens of others, as a citizen of the United States of America.

Despite my zeal for Americanization, German influences were still with me. I had German-Jewish relatives and friends, lived among German furniture and pictures, including the omnipresent painting of Speyer in my parents' living room, ate German-style foods, sang German songs at parties. And although I was an avid American Boy Scout, a member of the esteemed Order of the Arrow, my two closest scouting buddies were German Jews.

The year 1945 was a depressing one. I started college but didn't do well as a chemistry major, and then my grandfather died and I did even worse. I had resented my parents for putting him in a nursing home and felt that he died of heartbreak. Then when the war ended, my father got the official news about his sister and other relatives in the concentration camps.

After a year of college deferment, I was drafted into the army. I tried to be a good American soldier and came home on my first leave in impeccably shined boots and creaseless uniform. An acquaintance took one look at me and said, "You look like a genuine government issue—G.I."

The year in the army furthered my Americanization. Yet, afterwards I stayed best friends with a German Jew. But once I moved away from home after college graduation, German influences diminished. My new friends didn't know I was born in Germany, and when it came up I didn't discuss it. The eclipse of Egon and the gradual shedding of German culture had occurred almost unnoticed. But also unnoticed was the German childhood still inside me. It didn't surface again until twenty-five years later when, in 1979, Milly and I began to plan our first trip overseas. Then in 1983 uneasy plans for a trip to Germany took final shape. I wrote in my diary, "I am going back to a place that killed my friends and relatives!!" A few days later I wrote, "The desire to return to one's place of origin lurks deep . . . but they kicked me out . . . they murdered."

Until the day we left, my yearning to see the sites of my boyhood would surge, then falter, sometimes become enshrouded in a gray fog, sometimes almost die. "We'll just visit Lore," I said one day, "and we'll go to Speyer, but just run through, see my house and leave. Maybe Schwegenheim."

We chose a package tour that would give us the grand European vacation we wanted—Brussels, Luxemburg, Switzerland, Paris—and would also include some highlights of Germany. After the tour, we'd go back to Germany on our own. Milly and I sweated over how many days to stay there, finally narrowing it down to four or five. Then we argued about which it was to be!

"What would you do," she asked, "if you couldn't stand it and not be able to book an earlier flight out?" "*Schlag meinen Kopf an die Wand*," I joked. "I'd rather not hit *my* head against a wall," she retorted. We settled on four days.

At the airport on Friday, July 15, while waiting for our plane, I happened to open my passport. "Oh God," I blurted, slapping my forehead, "I took Walt's passport." It was lucky that the check-in clerk hadn't noticed the discrepancy. But what a stupid mistake especially after all my compulsive reviewing of our packing lists! "We might be held up in Brussels for hours," I whined.

I reached our daughter Karen and told her to express-mail my passport to the hotel in Switzerland. But I obsessed for the next two hours: What should I say in Brussels? Milly, unperturbed, said, "Play dumb."

The Brussels official said, "This is not your passport."

"Beg your pardon?" I asked.

"Not your passport; maybe your son's," he grinned, showing me Walt's photo.

I slapped my forehead, "Oh my God! I took the wrong passport!"

He advised we contact the American embassy on Monday. Later, our tour guide suggested I wait and see if the passport would arrive during our week's stay at a hotel in Switzerland.

That night I had a dream. I was in Speyer, just arrived, walking down a street, crying—crying for joy, and from sadness.

※ ※ ※ ※ ※

8

Yesterday's Fears

We had planned our trip wisely—a tour that did not plunge us directly into Germany, one that first gave us a pleasant visit in Brussels, a drive through the Ardennes woods, a stop in the quaint capital of Luxembourg. The scenery and the company of three dozen tourists put us into a vacation mood.

But the moment our bus crossed the border into Germany, my eyes moistened, my head bowed, and my voice quavered, "I am back." I stifled tears, not wanting to be overheard, and barely listened to the words of the tour guide, Peter, describing our next stop, the border town of Trier.

I peered out the window expecting to see something change because I was in Germany. Yet, everything continued to look the same as it had for the last few hours—until I saw a man in an undershirt leaning out the window of a factory building overlooking the road. I saw his crew-cut blonde hair, and imagined—or was it real?—a smirk on his face. *A Nazi!* my brain commanded.

Milly put her hand on my knee; I was trembling. As we neared the town, more people came into view, and I saw other

"Nazis." Peter was still talking but I remained conscious only of my own perceptions.

Milly shook me. The bus had stopped. A few moments later, only my awareness of the driver's outstretched hand and the fellow tourists behind me induced me to step off. Once on the ground, my feet became leaden. I turned to help Milly down. She looked grim.

As we walked hand in hand into town, I noticed that I was still wearing my tour I.D. tag. Impulsively, my hand whipped up and ripped it off. Stunned, I looked at my fist, realizing why my tag lay crumpled within: I did not want the Germans to see from my name that I am Jewish.

As I approached the picturesque town square, my feet moved forward grudgingly. Despite a blue sky with brilliant sunshine, the warm colors of the ancient buildings, the outdoor cafés, the fountains, the open air market, I felt chilled. Intense hunger drew my attention toward a tarpaulin-covered fruit and vegetable stand. I hesitated, then noticed an elderly man putting things into little brown paper bags the shape of which I had never seen before. Germans do come up with clever ideas! Those little bags are cone-shaped. They probably save paper, minimize crushing soft items. Then my eyes were drawn to a wooden box filled with ribbed yellowish-green berries. "Look, Mil, I used to love these as a kid. I forget what they're called in German. I think they're gooseberries."

We selected two tomatoes and two plums, and as the man put them into a cone-shaped bag I was about to ask him the name of the berries when he mumbled something. "*Das ist so wenig, daran kann ich nichts verdienen,*" I thought he said. Did I understand him right? "Too small a sale, I can't make money this way." No, my German is slow; or maybe he was kidding; or did he say it because I'm Jewish? I paid, and walked away confused between the sense of having misunderstood and the queasiness of doubt in my chest.

Milly went to find a bakery while I rested on the stone seat surrounding a fountain. I tried, like a tourist, to be thrilled with the splendid scenery but could not. Piercing voices of young German boys frolicking around the fountain pounded against my ears.

Milly returned with rolls, and we made tomato sandwiches. I took one bite and said, "German rolls are so good, so crisp. Not like the doughy stuff in America."

"Hmm," Milly murmured. She also still looked tense.

As the frolicking boys left, I whispered, "Did you find those kids especially loud, or is it just me?"

Milly found them loud, too. "Maybe it's the German language," she said.

"Or, let's face it, we're hypersensitive here."

"Maybe it's both."

We ate in silence for a while. Trying to lift our spirits, I commented "It's beautiful, though, isn't it? Look at the splendid colors on those buildings." But the words came out dull and flat. "What a paradox," I added somberly, "that human beings can create such beauty and do such ugly things."

We felt relieved as we got back on the bus. I wondered how the two other Jewish tourists felt but was too wrapped up in my own feelings to even ask. If I had, I might have become unwound, exploded.

Peter talked for a while, then said he'd give us a rest and come through the bus to answer our questions. I wanted to cry out, "Did you ever come across Jews who felt miserable when they reentered Germany?" The words stuck in my throat as he approached our seat. Why upset the other tourists? Maybe they wouldn't understand how I feel.

Peter passed by. On his way back, my throat became unstuck, and he addressed my question to everyone. Yes, other Jewish persons had told him how they felt when they entered Germany, he started, in slightly less-than-perfect English and his Swiss accent. "And some who were born there, or others who were born elsewhere in Europe, they have much feeling, some bitter. Of course, I sympathize with them. It was a terrible thing what the Nazis did. I was not there, not even born yet, and only understand it from the history books. And I believe very much in justice for all people and in peace and good relations between people. We really don't like to speak of such things too often; they happened, very bad unfortunate things and many people suffered. And I do not know how you can forget; maybe it is easy for me, and those of us who were not there and are not Jewish, to try not to speak of things that happened before I was even born; it is distant, a historical matter, but for those who had relatives in concentration camps, I'm sure they have much feeling, and have a right to such feelings." He thanked me for the chance to speak about the subject, hoped that since I was on vacation I could "enjoy something about Germany too, and enjoy the trip despite the many painful feelings I am sure you are experiencing."

In the quiet time that followed, I cross-examined myself. You knew you'd have feelings like this, Ed, so why did you come here? There are many Jews who wouldn't set foot on German soil. But now that you're here, what will you do with your feelings? Those people I saw as Nazis, they didn't really look like Nazis—and most were too young, or not even born until after the war. No, they're human beings, like me, with a different language, with some different habits. Different? I have some of those same habits! "You're a *Jäcke*," one of my German-born friends says, a perfectionist German.

Why did you rip your Jewish identity off your shirt? Why did you think the man in the factory building was smirking at you? Stop it. I know the answer. That paranoia goes back a long time. Only it wasn't paranoia then, it was real.

And in Trier I might even have passed some who had a part in it. But can I hold those kids around the fountain responsible?

There were Jew haters in America too. Think of the many times I was called a Jew as a kid, the snide remarks about Jews even during the middle of the war, and the time I was beaten up on the way home from Hebrew school. But does all that make it okay for me to feel good about Germans, about Germany?

Well you don't have to hate them. In fact you can't, Ed. You're you, an educated man, a Ph.D., steeped in sociology, social work, psychotherapy—and years of dedication to understanding people. You don't want to be a slave to your emotions. But do you want to stop feeling? No. But I'm going to also stand back and try to find answers.

Why did it happen in Germany? Should we blame *all* Germans? Shouldn't we blame the whole world? Human history is full of senseless killings, genocides. And yet, wasn't there something different about the Holocaust? I want to know more about the historical, sociopolitical, psychological, and other forces that brought it about.

Tired, I dozed, waking up when Peter started talking again. His words about the upcoming cruise on the beautiful Rhine brought a smile to my lips. My thoughts drifted to the Rhine in Speyer, its old pontoon bridge, the new embankment near our house that was to carry trains to a new bridge, the overpass they built that formed a sort of dividing line between my dirt street and the paved street that led into town. What was the name of my street in Speyer? I can't recall it. That's curious. Why didn't I look it up back home in my father's old papers?

It started to rain, then it poured, but it stopped just as the bus pulled up to the boat landing. "Now, enjoy the Rhine," I commanded myself. "Hitler didn't create it."

I felt moved by the charming panorama of castle-crested cliffs, terraced vineyards, timbered towns. As we passed the famous Lorelei rock, the haunting Lorelei song came to mind: *"Ich weiss nicht was soll es bedeuten, dass ich so traurig bin."* Its words fit my mood: "I don't know what it means, that I am so sad."

Further up the Rhine stood a charming little castle, painted red and white, right in the middle of the river. My heart leaped out to it as I saw emblazoned on it in big letters "PFALZ," the name of the province in which I lived as a boy.

The night's stopover was in Darmstadt, a city my mother had often referred to. I marveled at the friendly hotel, its gorgeous indoor pool, its sumptuous German meal. But a gray sadness still filled part of my brain when, at dusk, Milly and I went out for a walk.

During the night, I dreamt that I was in a German auditorium. A blonde middle-aged man was giving a speech to some young people in their twenties. The speaker, who was also the program's director, was boring, and he was cold, rigid, and dictatorial. I felt a responsibility to say something, but I was afraid of what would befall me. Another part of me did not care what would happen to me. Then I realized I was a foreigner, a neutral observer, and had diplomatic immunity. So at the end of the speech I got up and shouted, "This was the most boring speaker I have ever heard and the most rigid director I have ever met."

To my surprise, the audience did not attack me. It cheered. The director stood over me. I cowered, but thought: Is he a real threat? Then I saw in my hand a piece of glass—a glass brick. I smashed it to the floor.

Considering the dream, I wondered how many glass bricks I'd have to smash to see through to the fact that I am now immune to yesterday's fears. How many would I have to smash to stop feeling angry, suspicious, guilty?

The next day was my birthday, July 19. For this morning's destination, Heidelberg, I knew we would be passing near the area of my boyhood orbit. I craned my neck, wistfully trying to catch glimpses of familiar scenery. At Peter's mention of Mannheim, I jumped up to scan the horizon where he said it was located. I saw nothing. Shortly my heart leaped again. We passed a road sign "Speyer." Again I saw nothing.

In Heidelberg, I gaped at German trolleys, instantly associating them with my wonderful trolley rides in Mannheim from the train station to my grandmother's house.

As the bus strained up the steep, circular, cobbled mountain road to the famed Heidelberg castle, I seemed to recall being there once before, and found myself searching for the entrance to a cog railway which I was almost certain I rode inside that mountain, though I couldn't find a sign of it. While I enjoyed the lovely scenery from the terraced castle, I could hardly wait to get back on the bus, determined to search again for the cog railway on the way down.

As we rolled down the hill, my eyes stayed glued to the side of the mountain. Finally, I caught a glimpse of a small opening, saw tracks, and exclaimed, "There it is!" And suddenly I was about seven years of age, braced inside a little strangely shaped open car being pulled up, and up, very steeply, by some kind of chain making a loud burring and clackety-clack noise. And . . . yes . . . I had come here with my mother and Oma, but Mother was too nervous to ride on the cog—she always got sick on anything like that—so she must have hiked all the way up, and down too.

I breathed in deeply, smiling.

* * * * *

As we passed through the glorious Schwarzwald, I visualized a scene in the old family album, of myself about eight years old, in shorts, clamping a hiking stick, on a path in the woods, my father behind me.

In the small mountain town of Triberg, our tour group visited a souvenir shop known for its cuckoo clocks. At the entrance stood the owner, Willie Neff, a plump but solidly built man with gusty cheeks, a ruddy, radiant German face. He was holding a tray full of tiny plastic cups with different colored liquids. His dimples crinkled, his small wire-rimmed spectacles danced merrily, as he lilted, "Goot day ladies und gentelmen, vellcom to Villie Neffs, your frentli souvenir shop ver vee heff many beootiful tings verry vell made und guaranteed I assure you. Vellcom und come in, look arrount to your heart's content et all ze contents of our store. Und if you buy, do nott vorry how to pay; vee accept enny kind of money; trevelerrs shecks from all countries, personal shecks, cesh, bills, coins, American money, French, German, English." We laughed; then howled at his peroration, "Yes, ladies und gentelmen, vee take enny kind of money, vee take *aaaawwwlllll* your money.

"Und now ladies und gentelmen, vee hev some goot homemade vine for you," he concluded, handing out the tiny cups.

How could anyone not love the Rhine, the Schwarzwald, the friendly souvenir shop, I reflected, as we rolled out of town. Still, both Milly and I felt easier when we crossed the border into Switzerland.

* * * * *
9

Another Side of My Father

WHAT A CONTRAST Switzerland was to my mixed feelings about Germany! Here we breathed peacefully for ten days amidst scenes of white pillows of clouds gracing snow-capped mountains, we swam in tranquil lakes, delighted in thrilling chair lifts and charming train rides, and visited Geneva, the city where nations gather to reconcile. We ended our grand vacation tour in Paris and our spirits were high. But now I grew apprehensive about returning to Germany.

Our flight on the German airline was perfection—the cordiality, the cleanliness, the meals—and during our stopover at Frankfurt I was able to stretch out completely on a soft, upholstered lounge chair. Nowhere else is this possible, I thought, except in Germany. But I held back my enthusiasm. That same perfectionism had wrought the perfect machinery of destruction.

On the plane I felt an urge to start a conversation with my German neighbors. "I was born here too," I wanted to say. "I left here nearly fifty years ago." But I didn't talk at all. And as the pilot announced our descent into Nuremberg, I could not help thinking that here the swastika was in its glory, and my anxiety swelled anew.

In the airport terminal—a surprisingly small place for such a famous city—I felt like a nervous horse at the starting gate. Milly told me to slow down, so I sat and tried to collect myself while she picked up our baggage. I recalled the telegram we had received from Ernst, Lore's husband, a few days before we'd left for Germany: "Lore very ill. We will not be home." I had telephoned and learned that she had a serious case of arthritis and would be in a sanatorium several hours drive from her home. Yes, she cried, she would be so happy if we could visit her there.

Despite the terminal's relatively small parking lot it took me a long time to find the rental car, a nice bright-red Opel, and I was so nervous it took me twenty minutes to figure out how everything worked. Finally driving off, I found that I had to exit to the main road in order to return to the terminal, where I found Milly standing, all alone in front of the now closed building looking scared to death.

Soon we were on the famous Autobahn, planning to find lodging somewhere about halfway to the sanatorium in the village of Bad Abbach. My mind turned serene again, lulled by the charm of the Bavarian countryside. I felt almost good about being back in Germany! I liked the billboard-free Autobahn, noted how well the Opel held the road even when I tried it at the mad ninety miles per hour everyone else was doing. I noted colorful canvas-sided trucks, smaller than the monster trucks in the states but used in tandem.

Good ideas these Germans have, I thought, recalling my father's German curses at American-made products when he was frustrated, *"Unpraktishes Amerikanisches Ding!!"* I realized that I'd always liked things marked "Made in West Germany," automatically thinking they were superior to products made elsewhere.

Indeed, my connections with Germany were torn, but not broken. Yet, sad as I was that they were torn, I felt increasingly guilty about trying to mend them.

On a country road, I approached a German woman to ask about guest houses. She directed us to a town and waved cordially as we drove off, wishing us a good vacation. Entering the small town, I looked with nostalgia at the old German houses, the kerchiefed peasant women chatting in the little streets. A young motorcyclist went out of his way to lead us to the guest house. "Not the best," he warned us. Indeed there was a noisy tavern on the first floor and we drove back to the Autobahn.

We drove through to Bad Abbach, arriving at dusk. I misunderstood someone's directions to a hotel and drove around in circles till I found it. I gave my name, got the price for a room, and went outside to check with Milly. When I went back in, they told me they'd made a mistake. There was no room left. Because Stern is a Jewish name? my brain automatically asked. Or is my paranoia acting up again?

When I finally found a room, it was eleven o'clock. "It has been fifty years since I was here in Germany as a little boy," I said, checking in.

* * * * *

My heart pounded as I knocked on Lore's door at the sanatorium. It was opened by a short gray-haired woman. I instantly knew she was not Lore, despite my vague conception of my cousin.

Lore had been waiting for us since ten o'clock and might have already gone to lunch, the woman said as she led us through a long corridor to the dining room. "They are here, from America," she said to a man sitting in the hall outside. It was Lore's husband, Ernst.

Ernst was a short, soft-spoken man with a somewhat sad expression. He told us that Lore had started to get worried; she was looking forward so much to seeing me.

Then I saw Lore walking toward us.

"Egon, Egon," she wept.

We released our embrace to look into each other's tearful eyes, and embraced again. She was about five foot four, and if not in a weakened state she would have had a robust appearance. Her posture was still straight, and a warm kind smile must in better times have given radiance to the face that now looked intently at me. As we walked arm in arm to her room, I noted her stiffness and occasional shuffle.

She was feeling better, she explained, though a few weeks ago she thought she was going to die. She was always so strong, so healthy, till the sudden onset of her *Rheuma*. She recalled a picture she had given Walt last year during his visit, when she still had "red cheerful cheeks." Now she would be here for weeks, have treatments, including the sulfur baths the sanatorium is famous for, and perhaps another operation. Ernst had taken a room in town.

"I know your name is now Edgar," Lore said. "But can I call you Egon?"

"I'd love it," I blurted, surprised at myself for meaning it.

"Egon Stern," she said slowly, looking intently into my eyes. "You are a Stern. Just like me. We are Sterns. The Sterns all have something in common. Their eyes."

I looked at her closely, at the same time trying to visualize my father's eyes. Yes, my father's eyes did have a sort of prominence. One pupil off to the side—he never looked directly into a camera because of it—but it wasn't just that. I now remembered that his eyes shone.

"My father's eyes shone too. They were blue, and had a twinkle, like yours," Lore said. "We have Stern eyes."

I recalled the pictures of Aunt Anna, our fathers' sister, whose eyes actually protruded. I'll have to look those pictures up when I get back home, I reflected, puzzled that I had not thought of bringing them.

We talked through the afternoon, about the things people in an epochal reunion talk about—to review the past, to establish our present identity, to rebind our commonality, to reconnect. But this reunion was colored by the fact of our forced separation in an age when we had not expected ever to see each other again. I felt that we were both thinking about those terrible years in the mid-thirties and the horrible times that followed in Germany—the war, the camps, the burnings. And I was filled with an almost morbid curiosity, urgently wanting to know more about my family's experiences during the war. Since Lore was ill, I hesitated to press her with questions, but she told me a story I would never forget, about her father, my Uncle Willie.

Lore's mother, my Aunt Helene, was not Jewish, and for this reason, even though Willie maintained his Jewish ties, he was

The Peppermint Train

not deported at first. Lore did a lot to protect him, she said. I was curious about how, but her face told me she didn't want to talk about it.

Her father, an upholsterer, was put to work refurbishing German officers' furniture and automobiles. But in 1944, the Gestapo took him away.

Lore's voice lowered. "He worked for Eichmann," she said in a half whisper.

"For Eichmann?" I said, controlling my surprise, my neck tensing and my head cocking forward with curiosity.

"Yes," she continued, restrained, "for Eichmann. In Berlin. First he worked in his house, upholstering furniture. But after a week his officers thought it better not to have Jews in his house."

My eyes widened, and I nodded for her to continue.

"They put him to work cleaning stones."

"Cleaning stones?" I asked, urging her on.

"You know, stones." Lore said, making a brushing motion with one hand over the other.

"Yes, I understand." I said, "Stones. But what kind of stones did he clean for Eichmann?"

Stones and rubble near Eichmann's house, from the bombs, she explained.

Her next words startled me. "When Eichmann would come out of his house he used to leave cigarettes on the stones for the Jews."

It wasn't her words that startled me. It was her tone, as if to blithely say that Eichmann had some kindness in him. "His officers also left cigarettes on the stones," she said. "Yes, Eichmann was bad, but everybody has a little good in them."

I shot a glance at Milly. In the brief silence that followed, I pictured this man in his neat, brown, swastika-emblemed uniform, striding in highly polished boots past Jews on their hands and knees in ragged striped prisoner's garb, here and there laying a cigarette down.

I wished fervently that I could speak German with more ease. I might have said that with his damned cigarettes Eichmann got more work out of his Jewish slaves. Or I might have been speechless anyhow. And yet I couldn't help wondering. *Did* some of those murderers have some good in them? Could they have had a conscience?

"After a month," Lore went on, "my father was taken to Teresienstadt." When I asked what happened to him there, she said, very hesitantly, with sadness in her eyes, "*Gräber.*"

"*Gräber?*" I repeated, quizzically, recognizing the word for graves.

Lore motioned with her hands, to indicate shoveling. I understood. My uncle Willie dug graves in the concentration camp. Then, after the war, Lore said, Uncle Willie became caretaker at the Jewish cemetery in Mannheim. I shuddered.

* * * * *

Later, we all strolled on the beautiful grounds of the sanatorium. Lore stopped periodically in severe pain, and Ernst would pull at her arms to stretch them, which brought her relief. Whenever she rose from a sitting position she had to be helped up.

"Egon," Lore said. "You look so well. And your son Walter, he looks more like Milly, but he has beautiful curls like you had as a little boy. What happened to your curls?"

"Maybe you heard the story about my grandfather having them cut off when I was about five," I laughed. "But we must have seen each other after that. I was almost nine when we left."

"Yes, I was eighteen," she said.

"We were so overjoyed at Walter's visit last summer," she continued. "But he said he would write and we didn't hear from him." She chuckled, "Maybe he is like your father? He didn't write either."

We laughed as I acknowledged my father's dislike for writing. And I had a flashback to the time I was away in the service and I rarely heard from him and felt sad; and shortly after the war when I severely chided him for not writing to his niece, Gertrude—the one who had survived the concentration camp and got to Sweden. After the war, she had begged for replies to her letters, and Father always waited for months. But now, suddenly, hearing Lore's next words, I saw another side of my father: "But your father was always so helpful. He always sent packages and money after the war. Then he and your mother visited us in the 1960s." Yes, I recalled how conscientiously he packed those parcels and wrote out the money orders.

Lore reminded me that my father had been an avid mushroom collector. She had gone with him a couple of times. He would carry his mushroom handbook into the woods, rivet his attention to the ground, kneel and peer through a magnifying glass. He'd explain the differences between the poisonous and the safe ones. When he brought them home, everybody was afraid to eat them, but he insisted he knew what he was doing.

I remembered a day when my father and I bicycled into woods near Speyer and how much pleasure it gave him to show me the various mushrooms. I turned to Milly. "Isn't there a mushroom handbook somewhere on the shelf at home? I'll have to check when we get back."

We went to a charming garden café on the hospital grounds. I learned that Lore's mother lived in an old-age home in Mannheim. Lore told her about our visit. "We'll go see her if there is time," I said, and then spoke about how important it was for me to see Speyer. And Schwegenheim and Gommersheim.

"*Eine Wallfahrt,*" Ernst said.

The word *Wallfahrt* struck me. I hadn't called my trip a "pilgrimage" before. A pilgrimage is a visit to a holy shrine. But that was where I was going. Speyer was to me a holy shrine. I was on a pilgrimage!

* * * * *

When the waitress asked if we wanted dessert, I recalled having cheated on my diet in Brussels with Belgian ice cream and waffles. "For this reunion, I will cheat again," I said gleefully. "I want the best piece of chocolate layer cake you have."

She rattled off the names so fast I couldn't keep up with them, but I told her I wanted the one with nuts.

"Walnuts or hazelnuts?" she asked.

"Walnuts."

"With or without ice cream?"

I looked at Milly, my diet monitor. She left it to me. I put my hands on my stomach, smacked my lips. "Ladies and gentlemen I will now be a child again. Bring me a piece of chocolate torte with ice cream." We all laughed as I recounted the story of my Hanukkah torte in Hebrew school when I was six years old. "I got my torte then," I said. "I will have my torte now." I suddenly realized I had turned myself into Egon.

As we returned to Lore's room to pick up our things, a somber mood descended. No, Lore had replied, she would not be able to see us again tomorrow morning—she was scheduled for more tests. Lore and I locked in silent embrace. No one said a word about seeing each other again. I did not expect to ever again visit Germany. Outside her door, there was a final choked up *Aufwiedersehen*, and I turned, forced my shoulders straight, and walked stiffly down the corridor trying not to look back. I agonized. One more look? You might not want such a sad last picture. But it's not that, Edgar. It's something else. Are you afraid of crying? Like when Egon left his grandparents and Speyer forty-seven years ago?

* * * * *

The sadness about not being able to spend more time with Lore stayed with me. If only she hadn't been ill! There might have been so much more I could have learned from her about my family and the war. But why hadn't I ever asked my parents more questions when they were alive? They had gone back to Germany twice after the war. I even recall the bon voyage party on the boat in the 1960s. But I don't recall asking them much, if anything at all, about their trip. Vaguely I remember asking Mother if they saw Speyer, and she said "no," and that was the end of the discussion. What a silence there must have been about our past! Not until after my father died did I start to break that silence. Was it his passing, or was it merely the distance of time that enabled me to start looking back? Whatever it was, I now felt the need to know much, much more.

* * * * *
10

A Bridge to Home

It was five o'clock when we left Lore, and we could have reached Speyer by nine. But we needed to digest the past five hours before raising the curtain on another emotional scene.

We found a room in a pleasant small hotel with a patio restaurant. At dinner, an elderly couple at a nearby table helped us to translate the menu, and we ordered trout from the restaurant's huge fish tank. When I told the couple that I had left Germany "fifty years ago" and was going back to visit my hometown, they started to talk about the war. It was a terrible war, the woman said, very difficult for everyone, many people of all nationalities and religions were killed, food and goods were scarce, unavailable toward the end. From their generation, the generation that actually fought in the war, she told us, "those who have survived are not well—most of them are sick, of mind, spirit or body." She looked at her husband. "He is one of those who is not at all well. He spent time in a Russian prison camp."

The husband nodded sadly. "How is it in America," he asked. "Is the living any easier there?"

"We have our problems too," I said noncommittally, not

wanting him to feel I was better off even if it were true. Besides, I thought to myself, it seems pretty nice in Germany, less of a rat race, and people appear comfortable. "Each place has its advantages and disadvantages," I said.

"Have you ever thought of returning to Germany?" he asked.

"I made my home in America for almost fifty years," I replied diplomatically. "There are many things I liked about Germany and I've come back to see some of those things."

"Germany is a beautiful country," his wife said.

"Very beautiful," I nodded.

"Hopefully there won't be another war," the husband said, following up with comments about the world situation, the European, German and American economy, and the conflicts between the two superpowers. "In Germany we feel that Russia would never start a war," he continued. "There is more danger that America would cause a war to start." The next war would be a terrible thing, everyone concluded, and we should all hope for peace.

"Amazing," I later told Milly, "to have a friendly conversation with a man who might personally have killed American soldiers, or our Allies, or Jews." I wasn't feeling the kind of enmity that I felt in Trier, only more of a reserve than I normally accord strangers. "Two human beings caught in the Nazi madness," I added.

Milly looked stone-faced. They were two friendly people, she said, but her sympathy was not aroused by their talk of their difficult war years and subsequent sufferings.

Milly's right, I thought. How dare they complain, without even mentioning what their country did to us! But I stood back from my emotions and began to think. Had the couple built up defenses against facing their own responsibility? Had they really come to see their people as victims rather than aggressors? I couldn't reach such conclusions from the few words they had spoken. The more I thought, the more complex it all seemed. I certainly couldn't unravel it tonight, if ever.

I was too restless to sleep and stayed up a while to study our itinerary. Thoughts clashed in my mind. We had three days left, and there was so much I wanted to see. We could see Rothenburg tomorrow, I mused, the beautiful medieval town I was told we should not miss. It was on the "Romantic Road," not far out of our way, and I'd love to see it. No. Only three days left, hardly enough time for Speyer and Schwegenheim.

Even on the Autobahn the next morning, I was undecided until at the last moment I impulsively turned onto the exit "Romantic Road—Rothenburg." Shortly, a castle came into view. Should I take the time to see it?

"If we sit here undecided," Milly said, "we'll be wasting time."

I drove up, and from the castle garden's parapet, we viewed in silent awe a charming scene below—a town with sharply pitched tile roofs and a fairy-tale church spire nestled among green fields and rolling hills that floated into the horizon. This was the romantic, beautiful Germany.

* * * * *

After a quickstep tour of charming Rothenburg, Milly drove while I dozed and thought of my childhood haunts. And I wondered why, as urgently as I wanted to see Speyer, I went sightseeing today instead of going directly to it. I suspected that my trepidations had made me procrastinate.

At four o'clock I opened my eyes just in time to see a road sign "Mannheim/Ludwigshafen." My heart jumped. Memories swelled to the surface. Mannheim, my father's birthplace, where we used to ride the train and trolley to see his mother; Ludwigshafen, where he worked in the laboratory he would talk about with such pride. Mannheim—I still had his picture book depicting its prewar beauty and its postwar rubble. If only I had the time to see what the city looked like now.

Hands on the camera, ready to photograph the first road sign for Speyer, my heart raced when it came into view. "Slow down," I urged Milly, as the sign passed. I had forgotten to cock the shutter. My fingers trembling, I finally caught a sign: "Speyer, 25 km."

As we left the Autobahn, I let the camera drop to my chest. My back pressed against the seat, my hands clutched my thighs, my head craned in all directions looking for familiar landmarks. My body was rigid, my throat felt dry, and I felt a mixture of joyful and anxious expectancy. I would, after all my waiting, see Speyer again. Any moment now.

Poplar trees began to appear on the side of the road. I remembered them! There were many poplars in and around Speyer. I began to perspire. More and more poplars appeared. Suddenly, in the distance above the tree line I thought I saw two church spires. Could it be the Dom? Then, unmistakably, the spires and domes of the famous cathedral flickered between the trees. "The Dom, the Dom, there is Speyer," I cried, as a mixture of jubilation and intense sadness shot through me.

In a moment we came to a sign, "Rheinbrücke." I let out a terrible wail. It was the bridge across the Rhine! My face became a waterfall of tears. I cupped it with my hands, loosening my fingers only when I caught a glimpse again of the spires of the Dom as we reached the other side of the bridge. Then I quickly shut my eyes.

I asked Milly to stop. She parked at a gas station. I shut the window so I couldn't be heard crying, opened it again because of the heat. "Let's get the hell out of here," I snarled. "I can't go in."

* * * * *

The lines on the map weaved pointlessly before my weary eyes. Finally, the name of a familiar-sounding place came into focus. It was a sizable town to the south, where we might find lodgings.

Slumped silently in my seat, my half-closed eyes foggy, I watched the passing flat countryside. Soon I saw a small blue sign set on a low pole: "Schwegenheim." I looked toward the village and saw old houses. The lump in my throat swelled. I tried to visualize the dirt Bahnhofstrasse on which we lived. Then I saw a gas station. To my recollection, my little old Schwegenheim had no gas stations. As a boy I hardly knew what one looked like.

Shortly, our road passed through an old village. I again felt an incongruity. This macadam road on which cars and trucks rumbled constantly by the old houses was not at all like my childhood memories.

I heard a loud boom, soon another, and I saw trails of white smoke in the sky. Then I saw the jets. The map showed an air base in the place we were heading for. "We won't be able to sleep there," I groaned.

"Maybe we can at least get information," Milly said.

At the edge of town, the road passed over an expanse of train tracks. We parked at the little station, and I went in for something to drink. The middle-aged woman behind the counter looked at me rather intently, and I caught myself thinking again: It's because I'm Jewish. But when she poured soda into real glasses, I thought to myself: they do things right in Germany.

I brought Milly her soda, then tensely paced back and forth along the street. Should I go back to Speyer? Why did I cry so much when I crossed the bridge? Were they the tears Egon didn't shed forty-seven years ago? Yes, it was Egon who wept today.

"I'll drive," I finally said. "I'm ready to go home to Speyer."

* * * * *

The middle-aged man inside the gas station in the outskirts of Speyer sang a most gracious *"Danke Schön,"* as I paid him. *"Jawohl, jawohl,"* he chanted, when I asked about lodgings. "There is a hotel right down the street." He went to his desk to search for a pamphlet.

"Is that hotel expensive?" I asked.

"Today everything is expensive," he joked.

I asked about the one listed in my travel guide, across the river.

"That is more expensive," he grinned.

I asked where I could buy a map of Speyer.

"From me for free" he said, to my surprise.

At the hotel, the only room available was on street level. I was so weary I accepted it, though motorcycles and cars roared by. "The clerk said the noise would stop at seven when the stores close," I told Milly.

"When will it start in the morning?" she asked.

I quipped: "So it'll get you up for an early start instead of my having to shake you. I made it back to Speyer, we have two days left, and there won't be any late sleeping around here." But despite a lightening of my mood, I still felt an omnipresent undertone of apprehension and sadness.

The roar from the street brought back memories of a quieter Speyer, the sound of horses' hoofs and wooden wagon wheels, the farm across the street from my house, cobbled Johannisgasse. I thought of my parents' store, the post office, the Altpörtel. I searched my mind for where the synagogue used to be, and the fairgrounds. And I puzzled over why I couldn't remember the name of the street on which I had lived. I tossed from side to side on the bed, unable to rest. Finally I jumped up and began studying the map of Speyer.

The area where we were staying was unfamiliar to me, but it was not far from the center of town and the square where our store used to be. Now I could test the mental map I had drawn over the years against reality. My mind had altered a few details, but my map had been amazingly accurate considering the long passage of time. Nonetheless, I couldn't find the street where I'd lived.

As I studied the map again at dinner in the hotel's courtyard restaurant, a white-haired woman next to us offered help. I told her I had lived in Speyer, my parents had a store here and we emigrated fifty years ago.

"*Schade,*" she said.

Yes, I said to myself, it is "a pity."

"What happened in those years was so terrible," she continued. "But hopefully you will have a good reunion. Speyer is so pretty, and not changed much."

I told her I was looking forward to seeing it again. Meanwhile, a group of people in one corner were laughing raucously. Their voices echoed off the courtyard's wooden wall and stone floor. Once again a voice inside me cried out *Nazis*. Ridiculous, my rational voice objected. Those people are only having a good time. But my mood turned solemn as the suspicious voice spoke again. The waiter was keeping us waiting so long because we were Jewish. "Ridiculous," the rational voice countered.

Back in the room, Milly went right to sleep, but I studied the map again till my eyes started to close. I still had not found the name of my street.

* * * * *

The last time I had awakened in Speyer was early in the morning on June 29, 1936, dreading the farewells that were to take place that day. Now, early in the morning of August 2, 1983, I awoke again in Speyer, sad but also happy about retracing my boyhood. I mused on how the world had changed. In 1936 it took a week for the boat to cross the Atlantic; in 1983 it took a few hours by plane. In 1936 our letters took weeks; earlier this year I had telephoned Lore from New Jersey in less than a minute. In 1936, not everyone had a radio; now there were television antennas in the ancient villages.

What would Speyer look like? Was my house still there? Was my old neighborhood still rural? Was the Dom still surrounded by woods? And what about our store? I had heard it was still there, but it must have changed.

Studying the map again, I understood why my emotions had exploded yesterday as we crossed the bridge. It was the bridge that was under construction near my home in 1936, the bridge I had never seen completed—until yesterday.

Perhaps it was an uncanny coincidence, perhaps it was actually some unconscious knowledge that made me enter Speyer only a few blocks from the street where my childhood home was located, on the very embankment where I'd played "choo-choo" fifty years before. But for my street, the map showed a completely unfamiliar name.

I stepped into the shower. Why had I left this vital information at home? Maybe I really didn't want to go back there?

I tried the alphabet trick to jog my memory. At "M" I stopped. "Martin . . . Mac . . . Mark." I dashed from the shower to the map. I saw a familiar Lindenstrasse . . . then the Festplatz . . . then Markus-Strasse. "That's it!!" I shouted. "My street was Markus-Strasse." Only it was not on the other side of the embankment, and it was over a couple of blocks from where the train trestle used to be, the overpass that formed the entrance to my street. Something must have changed. Or my memory must be mistaken.

After breakfast, walking away from the hotel, my mood was like a hunter's, alert to every sight, sound and smell. Down the street were small old apartment buildings, colored in light grays, yellows. "My old Speyer," I sighed. Shortly, I saw a beautiful Gothic church. It looked familiar. Then I saw its name: Gedächtniskirche. Of course!

My spine began to tingle with a sense of expectancy. My feet carried me onto a "Gilgenstrasse," where, strangely, I thought, my nostrils caught a familiar scent. Then I gaped in amazement at the unbroken rows of houses on both sides of this curved street, each with a street-level store. It looked as if it hadn't changed in nearly a half century.

I stopped in a bookstore for a guidebook. "I lived here fifty years ago . . . my parents had a store down the street," I said to the young clerk. His face lit up, his voice became even friendlier and he asked my name so that he could put it on his visitors' list. As I paid for the book and some picture postcards of the city, I asked about a hotel. "There is a nice one down the block around the corner," he said, "the Goldener Engel."

Walking hand-in-hand with Milly, I saw, glimmering in the morning sun, the gray-brown baroque facade of the familiar post office. My feet slowed, as if to control my rushing emotions. I walked almost stealthily, as if in dramatic slow motion, zooming in on a pivotal scene of my boyhood. At the corner where Gilgenstrasse ended, my mouth opened, my spine tingled, my eyes incredulously beheld one of my boyhood's most familiar sights: the Postplatz—the central square of the town. I stood agape, feeling like I was saying hello to streets and buildings that were once my bosom friends. To the left was Bahnhofstrasse, the "Railroad Street" I used to walk so often to and from the train station. Across stood the impressive, stately German neobaroque, four-story Postamt. At the far end of the square, the tower of the Altpörtel rose into the air. And to my right, facing the post office, was my parents' former store, just as I remembered it: in a two-story building, the same large arched windows, one facing the square and two facing the narrow street that led to my home.

The air turned to silence in my ears; even the sounds of traffic were stilled. I had arrived at my sad, happy reunion.

I was amazed that the Postplatz was hardly changed; only more cars now, traffic lights and modern streetlights, maybe a few more advertising posters on the buildings but no evidence of neon. Suddenly I turned solemn. At the west wing of the post office just across from where we stood, I had a vision of a black boxy car standing there. It was waiting to take us away from Speyer. I heard a vague echo of heart-rending good-byes to my Oma and Opa in their nearby apartment.

I felt my knees tremble. Crossing over to the post office, I saw inside its open front door the familiar marbled steps that led to the service hall. "Let me sit here alone for a while," I told Milly.

Elbows on my knees, head on my hands, I stared across at what had been my parents' store. Instead of our name "Geschwister Walther," a sign read "CC Club Center." I could not make out what was in the windows.

A very impressive location, I noted—like Macy's on 34th Street. No wonder the store had employed over a dozen seamstresses and salesladies. My father had been planning to buy the building, and my mother once told me that there would have been money enough for my grandchildren.

Closing my eyes, I imagined my petite, springy mother waiting on customers, helping the salesgirls, sometimes scampering to the back room to adjust a hat, sometimes muttering something she could not say out front, and my father, more formal and distant, at the cash register or sitting over his ledgers in his little office in back. Then I recalled a scene from years later, in their small store in Washington Heights. My father had been laid off from his job as a packer in the millinery factory. I asked him why he wasn't out looking for another job. He yelled, "I always had a dream of having a big business." But the business in New York never got big. Sitting here now in Speyer, I finally understood what should have been obvious: the change from successful businessman to packer made him bitter and mistrustful. Now I could appreciate why he so often quarreled with my mother about their store in New York, which Mother ran. He felt more like an errand boy. But I also began to appreciate how hard he worked at whatever he could do. Even in his later years, when the millinery industry died and he could have just retired, he took a low-status job delivering securities on Wall Street.

Suddenly I visualized the beautiful arched windows across

the street plastered with anti-Jewish slogans, columns of men and boys in swastika-emblazoned brown uniforms goosestepping to the music of blaring bands through the arch of the Altpörtel. I felt a shudder of fear.

Now I remembered walking into the store on my way home from school, shortly before we left for America. My parents weren't there. I felt my face redden as a strange woman approached me and I realized that the store was no longer ours. "I am Egon Stern," I stammered as the new owner asked me what I wanted.

If only my parents were still alive, I thought, to answer the many questions racing through my mind. How did they feel at that time? What made them decide to leave while others stayed? Did they have to give their store away, or did they get a fair price for it? How much money could they bring to America? What station did Uncle Oscar drive us to for our train to Hamburg?

I took a deep breath and pulled out the picture postcards I had bought. I wrote one to Aunt Selma and one to a close friend who'd told me I would feel better as a result of my trip. Then suddenly I addressed one to myself.

> Dear Edgar,
> I was totally overcome with depression on crossing the Rhine bridge.... I couldn't take it all in at once, and had to get out of Speyer. This morning I am taking it in ... reliving ... my childhood hometown.... I am not depressed anymore, but sad and reminiscing.... I have returned!
>
>   Egon
>   Edgar

I strode up the steps of the Postamt, and as I asked for stamps at the counter I once again felt like I was Egon.

* * * * *

When I crossed the square, I saw that my parents' shop was now a bookstore. I stood and stared at it for a long time. Its glass entrance door, flanked by large show windows, appeared to be exactly the way it was in 1936; and there was the little back entrance which brought spirited memories. How often I had struggled to open that brown wooden door after school, sometimes rushing to the toilet at the end of the hallway. To the right, a step down, was my father's little office, then a room filled with babbling seamstresses pushing their needles, whirring their sewing machines, holding hats over hissing steamers, forcing hats onto bald iron heads that parted in the middle to make them stretch.

"Well," I said to Milly. "We're going into that store and somehow I'll get to see the back again, too."

But Milly shook her head. "Go ahead. I'll wait here."

I looked at her, puzzled, then shrugged and pushed open the door. Once inside, I felt tremendous joy, and disbelief that I was in my store again. It looked smaller. Along the walls were built-in shelves filled with books, and I could have sworn they were the same shelves on which ladies' hats used to hang over cute little cardboard cones. In back of the store was a door. It was open and I glimpsed a bit of the hallway. I had remembered correctly!

I controlled my urge to rush back there. The sales clerk was busy at the register. I waited till I couldn't wait any more and said *"Guten Tag."* I spoke my now well-practiced words about being back in Speyer after fifty years.

"A long time," she said with efficient German friendliness, bagging books for the line of customers.

"And you won't believe this," I continued animatedly, "but my parents had a millinery store in here."

Yes, she had heard it was a hat store once. That was before her time. It was a floor-covering business before the bookstore took it over.

I got rather animated telling her how exciting it was to be back. A couple of the customers nodded their heads at me. "And see if I remember right," I continued. "Through that door over there, then left was a toilet."

"Ja, ja, und ist noch dort," she said, now smiling directly into my eyes as the last customer paid.

"May I take pictures here, and go see the back?"

"Natürlich (Of course)," she nodded.

I went out to get Milly, but she said, "Ed, I don't want to hurt your feelings, but I really can't go into that store."

I swallowed. I was angry. There was something here that Milly couldn't face, and she wasn't joining me in my happiness. She must have been very uncomfortable for reasons of her own, but I had no idea what they were.

I went back in, took a picture of the door in back, walked into the corridor and turned left. There it was, that little door marked "Toilette." To its right was a small office, and a glass door led into a bigger room filled with boxes and stacks of books. That used to be the sewing room! I felt ecstatic. And sad.

I just had to buy something in this store. Anything. As I perused the shelves I was suddenly seized with a memory of my favorite childhood picture book. I rushed over to the clerk. "Do you have *Strubbelpeter?*"

"*Struwwelpeter,*" she corrected me. "Yes, but this is a club store and you need a card to buy it."

I went to look at it anyhow. I hadn't recalled how fantastic it was. It was an illustrated poem about "Unkempt Peter," a boy with foot-long nails he never cut and with a shock of uncombed hair that looked like a mass of tangled jungle vines. I vowed somehow, somewhere, to obtain *Struwwelpeter.*

At the register there was a bin of T-shirts with "CC Club Center" printed on them. Walt wanted a T-shirt with something on it from Germany. The clerk said I could buy shirts without a card.

I rejoined Milly, and I wanted to ask her why she hadn't wanted to go into the store with me. Something told me I'd better wait till later. I looked down the narrow side street I'd traveled so many times, and said half aloud, "Now I'm going to walk home."

My pace was brisk. Soon, we came to an old three-story brick school building. "Zeppelinschule" it said, over an arched entrance with massive twin wooden doors. They were the doors I walked through at the age of five with my terrified parents when they voted against Hitler! This was the school I later attended, until the Jews were thrown out.

I stared at the building, not so much with anger as with the past joy and sadness that it represented. When I walked into the yard facing the back of the school, a humorous episode came back to mind. One of the two back entrances was made of metal. How I remembered that metal door. It led to the boy's toilet. The toilet had a communal urinal with an awful smell that I hated. One day I decided to pee in the yard, and I got caught.

I walked over to some men eating lunch in a pickup truck parked near the back entrance. One of them had a weather-beaten face and white hair. He was at least my age. His wizened face didn't seem too eager for conversation, but when I told him I came to visit from America and attended this school fifty years ago, his eyes softened. He had gone to this school also. I asked about the school on Johannisgasse. He confirmed that children went for two years to that school and then came here.

He graduated in 1941 at the age of fourteen, he said. I was the same age, I exclaimed. We might even have been in the same class.

If only he were more talkative. If only I could find the right German words to ask more. But what would I ask? "How did you feel about Jews at the time?" We stood there for a few moments looking at each other. And I wondered what was going through *his* mind.

He turned to his men. "So, let's get on with the work."

"I'm amazed," Milly said, back on the street, "at the way you walk up to people here in Germany and simply start talking to them. You rarely do that at home."

"I'm amazed too," I said. And amazed at how much I don't say, I reflected.

Shortly, the street took a slight dip and fed into a short hill where three other streets intersected. I recognized the hill immediately. How could I ever forget it. I used to pump my *Vierrad* up this hill when I was about five and six and then gloriously race back down at top speed.

The *Vierrad* was a four-wheeler. Most people called it a *Holländer*. It wasn't an ordinary four-wheeler, but a fancy machine. It had a wooden bench seat on which I'd sit, alternately pulling and pushing a shaft that connected with a sprocket and chain which propelled the machine. It had hard rubber tires on spoke wheels that must have measured a foot or more in diameter.

The front end had a steering system that was operated by foot pedals. On the side was a brake lever, a bell, and a horn with a big rubber cup.

One day I was speeding furiously down the hill. As usual, when I reached level ground I kept on pumping ferociously to keep up the momentum. Suddenly I heard a clash of gears from beneath, the shaft felt loose, and though I kept pumping the machine came to a stop and would go no more. Instantly I envisioned my father scolding me for breaking my *Vierrad*. But instead he scolded about the mechanic who had fixed the machine not long before and then told me it was time, anyhow, for a two-wheeler. No, my father wasn't always a hard man, I now realized.

But I recalled the fuss about my learning to ride a bicycle. For reasons I never knew, my father would not teach me. Once at Aunt Selma's house he wanted me to go with a strange man who would give me a lesson. I just would not go. Father and Uncle Eugene at first asked me why, then yelled at me, until Mother and Aunt Selma told them to let me be. A while after that, I went with a nice man in Speyer to the Messplatz, where in no time I was riding my bicycle.

"We're getting closer to my house," I said to Milly, quickening the pace. A short distance ahead, I saw the embankment on which I used to play choo-choo hoping to see the first train come into the new little station next to the overpass—the train that, for me, never arrived. Suddenly I understood that I had come here hoping to see that little station again, and to see that train at last. But the embankment now carried a highway.

I rushed ahead hoping to find my street, the Markus-Strasse. But the sign read "Winterheimerstrasse." "I must be mistaken," I said. Maybe my street wasn't here. Yet, I could swear that the gray two-story apartment building here on this side of the embankment was the one I had passed every day.

For some unconscious reason, I did not venture through the underpass. Instead, I walked left two blocks. There, I found a "St. Markus-Strasse." I missed seeing the "St." on the map last night! And there's no underpass here. Besides, my street was on the south side of the embankment, this is on the north. Did they move the embankment? No, there are row houses here and other houses with cornerstones dating back to the 1920s. My street had only two houses—mine and a farmhouse across the way.

I was perspiring, feeling anxious, and very thirsty. We went into a little cafe, and while sipping a soda I suddenly remembered: my street's name was Markusweg, "Markus Way," not "Markus Street." "And my house number was 25," I blurted to Milly.

I rushed back to the underpass, walked through, but stopped. For some reason I still did not follow my instincts to walk straight ahead. Some inner force even overshadowed my rational thought that the street names had been changed.

I turned into a small housing development I'd never seen before, and greeted an old woman who was sweeping her sidewalk. "My name is Stern. I lived here fifty years ago . . . on Markusweg . . . my parents had a millinery store."

The old woman's shy eyes lit up. "*Ja,*" she nodded. "I still have one of those small hatstands from your mother's store," she said, "Geschwister Walther." I was flabbergasted. Her husband came out and when she told him what we were looking for, they chorused that the street names had been changed, that my house still stood. Exactly where I'd thought it was.

Rushing off, I wondered why I hadn't walked directly to it in the first place. It was only years later that I realized the obvious: I had procrastinated just as I had procrastinated in returning to Speyer. It was a difficult bridge to span, that bridge to home, that bridge of joy, of pain.

* * * * *

11

"We Were So Close, Your Family and Mine"

WHEN I SAW THE HOUSE, I could hardly believe my eyes. Although it had been modernized, it looked so much like I remembered it. It had a new coat of stucco, a different color paint, and the charming wooden shutters were gone, but above the entrance was the same prismed hexagonal window that used to fascinate me so. "It's the window in the stairway," I explained to Milly, reminding her that our apartment had been on the second floor.

Looking up, I described the layout of the apartment. The two windows of my parents' bedroom were to my left, two windows from the living room to my right, plus one facing the driveway. The kitchen was on the back corner, one window over the driveway and another overlooking the backyard. The bathroom was next to the kitchen—yes, I was sure, though I couldn't see it from the street, it had a little window out back. There was one other room in back that was Aunt Selma's bedroom for a while and then my grandparents'.

I hazily recalled sleeping in my parents' bedroom for a long time, then in a room on the third floor. I saw myself sitting on a bed reading *Struwwelpeter*. "It's amazing how much you remember," Milly said. "And you never talked about it."

I recalled the cast-iron wood stove in the kitchen, its roaring flames. My grandfather would lay raw potato slices on the top, let them bake to a crisp golden brown, cut them into small strips, then slide them into my mouth while bouncing me on his knee chanting, "*Hoppla Reiter, hoppla Reiter, hoppla hoppla hoppla Reiter.*" And I recalled the little woodworking projects Opa used to do on the oak table in the kitchen, like the plywood cutout now hanging in our dining room. "It's no wonder I decided to use that antique oak table as my workbench," I remarked to Milly, "although someone had offered a good price for it." I realized more clearly than ever that I loved using it because it belonged to my Opa.

"And I still have his *Hocker*," I said.

"*Hocker?*" Milly asked.

"You know, that blond stool with a seat that opens up to a little storage bin. I'll have to take it out of the attic when we get home."

I told Milly to wait, since I wanted to explore the house alone. I hesitated in front of the entrance door, uncomfortable with the thought that I was trespassing. The door was unlocked, so I took a deep breath and walked in. To the left were the familiar steep stairs to the cellar, and I recalled how my little Oma used to struggle helping me carry my bicycle up those steps. Now I softly tiptoed down, anxious to see what I would find. No more black coal pile! No more potato sacks! Just a huge boiler system with brass and silver colored tubes, valves, and gauges.

Too excited to take a picture, and too anxious I stayed only a few seconds, but during that moment I had another flashback. I was about four. It was close to Christmas. A man came to the house looking like *St. Nickolaus*. He was in a red suit and carried a big sack over one shoulder. He had a deep voice. "If you are good, you will get nice presents," he said. "But if you are bad," he boomed, winking at Oma, "I'll come back and lock you in the dark cellar. Ho, ho, ho."

I smiled, recalling how genuinely frightened I was for days. Oma had to reassure me the man had said it in fun. Besides, I was a good boy.

I tiptoed up the stairs to the landing of the first-floor apartment, thinking of the playmate that used to live there, then softly bounded up two steps at a time to the door of my former home. I heard voices inside. What if someone came out? I would be shy, afraid. Don't be ridiculous, Ed, I said to myself. I'm not Egon anymore. Just tell them I lived here fifty years ago.

I turned, too overwhelmed to think clearly, and climbed the steps to the third floor, expecting to see a hall with a door to my former bedroom. The hall was gone. The whole third floor was now one apartment. On the way down, I paused to stare at the sunlight glistening through the prisms of the octagonal stairwell window that had fascinated Egon.

Outside, I looked for the garden. It was gone. And on the north side of the house was a parking lot where once there had been all wild growth. I observed that this north wall of the house had no windows—that it was actually the back of the house—and sadly noted that there was a billboard on it.

We peeked into the backyard. There was no fence, and I could have walked in. But I didn't. There was a patio with a fiberglass roof, a small patch of lawn. "This used to be all bare ground," I said, almost with a pang of annoyance that my old house had been made to look so sleek. But then I giggled, "At this corner was the little chicken house." I could see myself on my hands and knees, crawling through the straw to fetch the eggs.

A quacking goose echoed in my mind. Oma was chasing the goose, Opa flourishing his cane to shoo it toward her, Oma grabbing it by the neck, scooping up handfuls of dried corn from her apron and forcing it down the bird's neck until no more would go down. I felt sorry for that goose even now. When it was fat enough to be eaten, Opa would cut its neck. I could never look. Then Oma would sew something together when she prepared it for cooking. I'd never eat it, or any other fowl. My excuse—which became a family joke—"it was sewn together."

They never forced me to eat fowl, but Mother and Oma used to cook a soup which was the bane and torment of my German childhood. It was called *"Grün Kern Suppe,"* made from some kind of green barley. I detested that soup and could even now picture Father sending me out of the kitchen to sit at the little foyer table to finish my bowl of *Grün Kern Suppe* before I'd be allowed to come back for the main course. Did I associate those kernels with the ones they stuffed into the goose?

"Well," I said to Milly, "the afternoon is moving on. There's lots more to see. Let's go down to the pond."

The pond was only a minute's walk, much closer than I had remembered. When I saw it, I was awestruck. It had become a gorgeous little lake lined by huge shade trees and benches. Even Milly, who had so far expressed almost no enthusiasm for anything, burst out, "How pretty."

"I don't think it was this way in the thirties," I said. "It looks like they made it into a park."

A couple was coming back from a walk around the lake. I spoke my usual greetings. They had lived all their lives in Speyer, they said. They know a Jewish couple who moved to California, and a person who comes back periodically to visit the Jewish cemetery. I was surprised that there was still a Jewish cemetery here.

Milly and I went to sit under a tree, ate our lunch and fed the ducks. Then I sat staring at the water. The water turned to ice. I saw children on skates, some on wooden-runner sleds. Aunt Ingrid, Uncle Oscar's wife, had urged my parents to let her teach me to skate. Even now, feeling the warm sun shimmering through the trees, I wondered why they never let me.

I noticed the houses on the south side of the lake. They didn't look very new. There must have been more houses in this neighborhood back in the thirties than I thought. Nevertheless, it was still my rural Speyer. Maybe today they would call it suburban.

As we walked the path around the lake, I began to search for the house in which my playmate Klaus used to live. I hadn't seen it across from my house, but maybe it was still there, behind the day-care center and the greenhouses that now replaced the potato field of my childhood days. Suddenly I saw something familiar between the trees—a yellowish stucco house. My heart beat faster, and I trotted to the street. In front of the day-care center I waited for Milly and struggled to recall my playmate's last name. Using the alphabet trick, I stopped at "H." Just then Milly came to my side and I cried "Härter!"

82

I dashed ahead again and turned left at the corner. There, about a hundred feet down a driveway, stood the Härters' house, almost exactly as I had remembered it. Even the color looked the same. Only the porch was changed. Five or six people were talking in front of the house. I stood a few moments, unsure what to do, and finally walked down the driveway. One of the men asked if he could help me.

"Does a Mr. Härter still live here?" I asked.

"Yes, I am Mr. Härter," the man said.

"My name is Stern," I said. "I used to live across the street."

He looked at me closely for a second, broke into a broad, inviting smile and shot out a hefty hand to grab my arm. "Egon Stern?!"

"Yes, I am Egon," I replied, trying to contain my excitement.

"And I am Konrad. You must stay and visit. I'll be finished with these people in a few minutes."

I went to get Milly. As the people left, Konrad virtually crushed my hand in his. "This is quite a surprise, Egon. I am Konrad, brother to Klaus. You remember Klaus. He was your playmate." Konrad took us into his house, beside himself with happiness, and introduced his wife. I felt almost speechless.

Konrad had a face that reached out to you, with warm inviting eyes and friendly dimples, and a robust build that belied his age. He was fifteen when I left in 1936, he said. "And you and Klaus were born within two weeks of each other."

"Incredible!" I exclaimed, flabbergasted at the chance to peek into this long-forgotten friendship.

"And Selma," he said, with obvious fondness. "What ever happened to Aunt Selma."

"She is still living," I told him.

"I remember her so well," he continued. "She lived with you for a while. Your family lived on the second floor. My family lived on the third floor."

"That's astounding!" I exclaimed. "I never knew that."

"Yes, Egon, our families were very close," he said. "We lived in the same house till 1932 when my father built this house."

"And it's exactly as I remembered it," I said. "Except the porch is different, isn't it?"

"You remember well. We enlarged the front."

He turned to Milly, asking if she understood what we were saying.

"*Ein bissel*, a little," Milly chuckled, explaining with my help that she knows Yiddish, which is a bit like German.

"I have old pictures at home of the potato field," I said. "And of our families in front of your house."

"We were so close, your family and mine," said Konrad. "My mother used to help in the hat store. In fact, she helped your mother pack your steamer trunk when you went to America."

"Really!" I exclaimed. "That trunk is still in our attic."

"How often I told my children the story about your family," he continued. "I lectured them about our history, about how I predicted that bad things would come from the Nazi regime. In 1940, the Nazis came and conscripted me too."

There was a moment of silence. Would I ask the questions that shot through my mind if I could speak German more fluently? Is Konrad saying he was not a Nazi, that he did not want to go into the army? Was he for Hitler?

Mrs. Härter asked if we would have coffee and cake. "With pleasure," I said quickly, hoping Konrad would continue, which he did.

"I was away for ten years. Seven of them in a Russian prison camp, mostly in Siberia. Most men didn't survive there. I had a good constitution."

Konrad called my father "a clever, judicious man." My mother and Selma didn't want to go to faraway America, he told me, only to France or Holland. "But your father saw what was coming and told everyone that the Jews have to go far away from Germany. You were lucky that he was stubborn as well as shrewd. Many others weren't so lucky." Suddenly I felt a pang of guilt for looking down on my father all these years. Even the fact that he had had a big business and gave it up to take us to safety was a relatively new idea to me.

"I always wondered what happened to you," Konrad said, "and why nobody ever wrote."

A quick succession of thoughts and feelings shot through me in the few seconds of awkward silence that followed. I really knew nothing of how my parents felt about the friends and neighbors they left behind. I didn't remember their ever writing to anyone. And did Konrad recall that Klaus stopped playing with me after the Nazis came to power?

I motioned with my hands and shoulders, not knowing what to say, then started, "People get busy with their own lives." But that's not honest enough, I thought, considering Konrad's apparent sincerity. "Some people," I continued, struggling with my German, "especially the older generation, they have some, some feeling, how would you say it. . . ."

"Resentment," Mrs. Härter said in English, nodding empathetically.

"Yes," I nodded slowly. We looked at each other. "It's a sensitive topic. What can one say."

Mrs. Härter left the kitchen and returned with a photo. Standing in front of their house on the potato field were Konrad, Klaus, their grandmother, their parents, Aunt Selma and myself. "I'd like you to have this picture," Mrs. Härter said.

It's the same photo as in my album, I knew, but trying to be diplomatic, I accepted the gift.

I talked about how nice the neighborhood still looked.

"And did you go down to the Russeweiher?" Konrad asked.

"Russeweiher?" I repeated. "Oh, yes. That's what the pond was called! Yes, the Russeweiher. It's so pretty now. Russian pond, it's called," I said to Milly.

Finishing our cake and coffee, I remarked about the hour and said we'd have to go soon.

"Do you want to see Klaus?" Konrad asked. There was a hesitancy in his voice and for a moment I wondered if he was thinking I might not want to see Klaus because he'd stopped playing with me. Konrad might not recall that, but surely he'd remember if Klaus had joined the Nazis! Nonetheless, though tired and hungry, I could not turn down this incredible opportunity.

"Well, we've been walking since eight this morning," I said.

"I'll drive you over."

Klaus and I must have stopped playing together when we were five or six, but living so close, I reflected, we must have seen each other till I left. Yet he remained only a name in my mind, despite the photographs. Did he really join the Hitler Youth? Lots of kids did. They joined for the fun, not for the ideology. What does a young kid know about ideology? But where did his family stand? How did they vote?

I wasn't sure how I should feel. Could I reconcile reestablishing relationships here with my resolve never to forget the Holocaust? The photo of Klaus and me on the potato field came to mind. Yes, I did want to see him. Furthermore, I'd promised to keep an open mind, to learn something.

When we arrived at Klaus' house, Konrad burst in without knocking. "I brought you some visitors," he cried. "I didn't call because I wanted it to be a surprise like it was with me. They are from America. Someone you used to know."

Klaus and his wife looked up from their dinner.

"His name is Egon!" Konrad added, dramatically.

Klaus blinked several times from behind large-frame glasses. Slowly, he rose, peering at me. He forced a smile, tensely breathing *"Das is der Egon?"*

"Ja, Egon Stern," Konrad said.

"Yes, I am Egon," I said.

"Really Egon?" Klaus said, still in disbelief.

"We were such close friends," we said, almost in unison, shaking hands.

Klaus was tall and lean, well tanned, athletic-looking, more reserved than his brother, even circumspect. As words slowly broke through our speechlessness, and with the help of Konrad's vivacity, we began to reminisce about our families, about Speyer. From Konrad there seemed to be no restraint—he seemed to enjoy himself, and I enjoyed him. But with Klaus, I was more hesitant—maybe in response to his quieter personality, maybe in response to the questions I was suppressing in the joy of this reunion.

Klaus remembered as little about my family as I remembered about his. We were both young. But we painted vivid scenes about Speyer.

"Do you remember the Messplatz?" Klaus asked.

"Natürlich," I said. "How could I ever forget it. Is it still there?"

"Yes. It's smaller now," he said, "but they have a fair every year just like they used to." Klaus also recalled the pontoon bridge. "When a train went on it, the pontoons would sink down into the water, then swoosh back up. Remember how we used to love that?"

"It was dismantled in 1938 when the new bridge opened," Konrad said.

The bridge I never saw.

"We used to play on the embankment up the street," Klaus said. "Before the trains started running."

The train I never saw.

"In 1945," Konrad said, "the bridge was blown up as the Americans headed for Speyer."

I felt a pang of sadness that the bridge I wanted so much to see was blown up—paradoxically, by the Germans. I imagined the American soldiers entering Speyer and building another pontoon bridge across the Rhine. I felt the irony of my being here, an American, in the home of former German friends. I suppressed a surge of vindictive joy that I was on the side of the victors, they on the side of the losers. I wondered what was going through *their* minds.

"Speyer was not damaged during the war," I heard Konrad say. "It now has twice as many people: 50,000."

"But it is still charming," I said. "Most of the buildings look the same."

"Yes," Klaus replied. "We try to restore buildings instead of tearing them down."

"Yes, yes," Konrad suddenly sighed. "Good and bad times there were during our youth."

When we left, Klaus's gift bottle of wine under my arm, I felt happy. I reflected that my family had never said anything bad about the Härters, at least not that I could recall. Even the references to Klaus joining the Hitler Youth were made with sadness rather than rancor. And tonight I had sat with them, former neighbors, two human beings who willingly or unwillingly, and I really don't know which, were on Hitler's side.

The doubt and underlying sadness reemerged. Was it from that which had not been spoken? And why hadn't the Härters asked for my address? I'd asked for theirs.

* * * * *

When we arrived at the Goldener Engel Hotel, I suddenly realized that the hotel was on the very street where, forty-seven years before, I was torn away from my grandparents.

I was tired. Milly was too, but more than that she looked extremely tense. We flopped down on the bed without unpacking or even speaking.

Shortly I was up again, feeling compelled to walk alone down the Bahnhofstrasse to the train station. I walked briskly, eager to see the Speyer station again. Passing an apartment house, I suddenly stopped. The last time I passed this house I was about eight and had an upset stomach. I rang the bell of a boy I knew. His mother said that Jews have to use their own toilets.

I walked on now, slowing my pace with nostalgic expectancy as I approached the train station. It had not changed! Only it looked smaller. No, it was I who had gotten bigger.

I examined a train schedule, wishing I could board a German train again. If only there were time, I could take the train to Ludwigshafen, then ride the trolley to Mannheim. The Peppermint Train was gone, I knew. I scanned the tracks, wondering where it used to be waiting.

* * * * *

At about eight, after we'd rested, I asked Milly about her reactions to the day's events.

"Uncomfortable," she replied.

"How about the visit to the Härters?" I asked.

"I could begin to see human beings," she said, crisply.

"Anything else?" I asked.

Milly was silent. I waited, tensely.

"What were *your* reactions," she finally said.

I clenched my jaw, then blurted, angrily, "Why are you asking about *my* reactions. All you've said so far is a few words!"

There was a heavy silence. Milly started to cry, then asked why I was angry.

"Why didn't you go into the store with me?" I asked.

"I couldn't," she muttered.

"Do you know why?"

"Because of what they did to you and your parents," she said.

"Anything else?"

"No!"

"Maybe we should just go and eat," I replied.

As we walked away from the hotel, the tension became unbearable. I decided it would be best to go off by myself. "I might be back late," I said. Then I walked down the main street, heading for the Dom.

Dusk was settling in. Speyer had gone to rest. The Altpörtel's illuminated clock shone pleasantly down at me. Centuries-old buildings glowed calmly in the twilight, still awake with softly lit store windows displaying things like those I used to see as a boy—clothing, toys, chocolates—and things that as a child I never dreamed of—electronic toys, TVs, computers. Then the peacefulness of the old town was suddenly jarred by the roar of motorcycles, and when I saw a McDonald's I realized that while still quaint, my Speyer had entered the modern world.

The lights of the Dom were already lit, casting a mellow glow on its imposing Romanesque facade, its three huge portals, and the two front towers between which reposed its octagonal dome. My skin tingled as I walked past the church into the woods. It was a sort of wooded park, with trails. Here and there was a lamppost, and the illumination cast eerie shadows on the massive sides and rear of the cathedral.

As I strolled in the semidarkness through the deserted woods toward the Rhine, I became afraid. Then I heard German voices in the distance and began to tremble. In a moment I saw a softly lit refreshment booth. Young people were gathered around it. I felt my body shrink.

"Edgar," I almost said out loud, "this is 1983, not 1936!" I walked to the booth, stood among the young German people, and bought some picture cards.

As I arrived at the Rhine, I found a quietly lit terrace restaurant overlooking the river. I took a seat and stared blankly into the night, gradually becoming conscious of the sights around me. Below the terrace, a wide cobblestone street sloped down directly to the water. Perhaps this is where the pontoon bridge used to be? I became aware of an excursion boat docked a few hundred feet away. In the shifting breeze, I heard undulating waves of German music and singing, intermingled with the gentle lapping of the river against the softly swaying ship.

While sipping a beer and waiting for my meal I began to think again, and I filled pages in my diary. I puzzled over Milly's discomfort with Germany, her refusal to go into the store with me. I recalled others asking me why I was going back to Germany. I'd replied that I had some fond connections there. I recalled some of Milly's remarks while we were planning this trip. "Of course," I wrote. "She never had any positive connections here. She associates Germany only with the murder of six million Jews and what befell me and my family." My heart, on the other hand, is torn between the pain of that horror and my intimate, emotional connections here. But why is she so adamant?

Suddenly I became conscious of the lights twinkling on the Rhine Bridge, and their reflections dancing in the water below. This is the Rhine, I reminded myself, a beautiful river, not made by evil men. May I at least unambiguously love the river I once loved?

* * * * *
12

A Cathedral, a Synagogue, a T-shirt

On our fourth and last day, I awoke feeling overwhelmed by all I still wanted to do: tour the Dom; find the site of my former synagogue; see the Messplatz, Johannisgasse, and my first grade school; visit Aunt Helene in Mannheim; and, above everything else, go to Schwegenheim, find my grandparents' house and the site of the Peppermint Train, and walk in the woods. And I wanted to at least drive through Gommersheim, the site of my chocolate farewell. I wished now that we had scheduled that fifth day.

If only there were time to go to Kaiserslautern, to Dolgesheim, to Seeheim, I reflected. And I came all this way to Germany and would not visit a concentration camp. "Too painful," I had said, while planning the trip.

As Milly and I deliberated about how much we could fit in, she said, "There's one thing I definitely want to do. I want to find Walt the T-shirt he asked for."

"But I bought him one that says CC Club Center," I said.

"But that's not German," Milly said.

"How German does he want it?" I said, sarcastically. "I won't have my children wearing anything *too* German!"

* * * * *

Today, I noted that Speyer had changed after all. It had the noise and stink of traffic, big stores, quick eateries, and other accoutrements of a contemporary city. But it still had charm: the Postamt, the Altpörtel, quaint cobbled alleys with little stores, sidewalk cafés—and the majestic Dom, facing the end of the main street.

As we walked toward the cathedral, we hurried in and out of stores looking for Walt's T-shirt but to no avail. Then, despite my rush, I walked into a candy shop that sported a sign *"Diat Chocolat."* It had the largest display of diet chocolates I had ever seen: dark chocolate and light chocolate; various nut-, fruit-, and creme-filled chocolates; truffles; chocolate-covered pretzels. All sizes and shapes in deliciously colorful wrappers: bars; boxes that were square, round, heart-shaped; pictures of white-wigged princes and princesses on foil-wrapped rum balls, a horse-drawn sled on truffles, a choo-choo train on marzipan bars.

I selected two cartons full of treasures while Milly hunted for T-shirts next door. She came back empty-handed, and we left the chocolate for later pickup and rushed to the Dom.

The Romanesque cathedral shone magnificently in the morning sun, and the wooded park looked lovely. The Dom had "a completely new appearance," the guidebook pointed out, "from the restoration in 1961." But despite its new, clean, brick face, the basic structure was the same: four towers, an octagonal front dome, a bell-shaped rear dome, and massive doors that I remembered well. As we walked through them I formed a vague image of entering this church once before, with my mother. I think it was a wedding—perhaps of one of her salesladies.

If I had thought the cathedral huge then, its starkly plain, almost austere straight lines and unadorned arches gave it an upward sweep that even now made it look like the tallest church I had ever seen.

Milly's face looked as austere as the church. She said she wouldn't go see the rooms where the Kaisers were buried. But for me, the Dom was a monument of my childhood. Besides, I wasn't going to shun its crypts any more than I would shun the crypt of a Pharaoh who made the Jews' lives miserable. Avoiding these things wouldn't help me to understand anti-Semitism and the Holocaust.

Later, walking in the wooded park, Milly conceded, "I can see why you were so fond of this place. It *is* beautiful."

We started back into town to find the site of my former synagogue. In contrast to my objectivity about the cathedral, discovering the site of the synagogue seared my soul.

I had an idea of where it should be—on the south side of the main street, not too far from the store. We walked in that direction, on a narrow street—an alley—named Judengasse.

"Judengasse means Jew Street, or Jews' Street, or Jewish Street," I said to Milly.

"We saw one in Rothenburg too," she reminded me.

"There must be one in every town in Germany, maybe all over Europe," I observed.

"Reminders of ghetto life," Milly said. "I wonder if the Nazis tore the Jew Street signs down during the war. Wouldn't it be an odd paradox if they'd left them up?"

We came upon an ancient mikvah, now a historical site. "A Jewish ritual bath, not destroyed by the Nazis?" I said. Then I recalled that there were still Jewish cemeteries in Germany, too. The gate of the mikvah was locked, but a notice directed where the key could be obtained. Just then, another visitor happened along with the key, and we offered to return it.

On the remains of the ancient wall surrounding the grounds was a large plaque with a lengthy inscription. Struggling to translate it, I gasped when I saw the words "destruction of the synagogue." The sign darkened in my eyes, every muscle in my body strained, my throat parched in the hot sun. Is this the spot where my synagogue was burned down?

A hazy scene of a Saturday morning service rolled through me. The rabbi announced the last hymn. Egon came to the bimah. He sang, *"En . . . ke . . . lo . . . he . . . enu. . . ."* The congregation joined in. Egon's family watched him, proudly.

Through tears, I read on, about the origin of the mikvah, the Speyer Jewish community, its unfortunate destruction.

Another couple entered the grounds. They were considerably

younger than we, and I was curious why the woman, who appeared Jewish, looked so solemn. I wanted to approach her to ask what memories she was looking up, to hear of her sadness, to tell about mine. But she never looked at me, seemingly absorbed in her own feelings.

Milly went down the steps into the ancient mikvah, but I wasn't interested. I was obsessed with whether my synagogue had really stood here.

These grounds just didn't look familiar. Then I noted on the inscription that the synagogue on this site had been an ancient one and that a new one had been "rebuilt in another location." Later, when I returned the key, I asked the man behind the desk where the last synagogue had stood.

The man's face, and voice, seemed deliberately sad, as he replied, *"Das war an Heydenreichstrasse."*

I located the street on the map. It was closer to our store, just as I had thought. I rushed ahead, my heart beating wildly. I immediately recognized the small square, on one side a stone wall surrounding an open area, opposite a narrow intersecting street called Hellermanstrasse. Yes! My synagogue was at this little square, on Hellermanstrasse.

The hell that I escaped.

My eyes danced nervously around the square. As I looked down the little street toward town, I recalled the movie about Palestine, my father selling tickets—it was down that little street I ran, holding on to the big bill he gave me to get more change.

Suddenly, I saw on the wall of a warehouse across the square what looked like a bronze plaque and walked over to it. My face was taut, my body rigid, as I translated it:

> HERE STOOD
> THE SYNAGOGUE OF THE
> JEWISH
> CONGREGATION OF SPEYER
> UNTIL ITS DESTRUCTION
> BY THE NATIONAL SOCIALISTS
> IN THE NIGHT OF
> NOVEMBER 9–10, 1938

Perspiring as if standing in front of those flames, I tried again to form an image of the synagogue, but none came. I jerked myself away from Milly. "I can't stand it any more. I've got to get the hell out of here," I said. But I was unable to move.

"Let's find a place to sit down," Milly said, taking my hand. "You're very upset. It's hot. Don't overdo it."

Abruptly I darted down to the main street. We walked into a pleasant café. Its garden setting contrasted so sharply with my agitation and sorrow, I burst into tears. As I fled to the men's room, my brain screamed: So many burned. And I am alive!

A few minutes later, pensively sipping on a cold soda, I said to Milly, "Something big is happening to me on this trip."

Yes, I thought, something is happening to me, and there are going to be some changes in my life. "I'm in the wrong job in that damned clinic," I blurted.

"I've felt that for a long time," Milly said. "But is that what's really bothering you right now?"

No, I reflected. I need to find out more about all that happened to me, to my relatives, to so many—and to understand.

* * * * *

It was one-thirty. The rest of the day's itinerary pressed on my mind. While Milly resumed her quest for a T-shirt, I dashed to the Johannisgasse in the old section of Speyer. This narrow ancient street was now paved, its continuous row of original houses restored, the old look gone. An occasional car roared by. Still, I felt some of the tranquil charm of fifty years ago. The sidewalks were still cobbled. The old church tower still inspired the scene. The tower was painted a bright white, and its narrow vertical stained glass windows flanked by two round clocks gave it the appearance of a face smiling down on the neighborhood. On top of this face, two black-roofed twin cupolas sat one atop the other, beckoning with their pinnacle into the peaceful blue heaven.

Although the quaint wooden street-wagons shown in my living room painting were gone, luckily no cars were on the street as I photographed the scene from the same vantage point from which the artist had painted it.

I rushed down Johannisgasse to find my first grade school,

only to see a pile of rubble and a sign announcing the school's removal. Yet, a huge old oak tree prompted a vague memory of the way the yard and the building had looked. Then my head turned instinctively across the street to the old rowhouses. They had been modernized, but I instantly recognized the one with the driveway where I used to leave my bicycle—until the family no longer dealt with Jews.

Back in our room, Milly told me that she could not find T-shirts with anything German imprinted. "But the hotel manager told me that one of the Speyer papers was selling such shirts at one time," she said, smiling broadly.

I agonized. Milly should enjoy something too, here in Germany, but she's worried about bringing home a lousy T-shirt when time is pressing in my head for doing what I came for!

"I want to see what they're like," Milly said.

Wearily, and weakly, I pleaded, "I'm debating whether there's even time to visit Aunt Helene in Mannheim."

"And you need a rest before we do anything else at all," Milly said.

I lay down, but tossed, debating about seeing Aunt Helene. If I telephone her, she'll surely ask me to visit. And I have to get to Schwegenheim. But Mannheim was only half an hour's drive, so I picked up the telephone and dialed.

Aunt Helene was delighted that we would visit.

Relieved at my decision, I did my relaxation exercises for fifteen minutes, showered quickly, and we rushed out of the hotel at three o'clock, stopping in town for the T-shirts. I waited by the car for what seemed like an eternity, and on Milly's return I sped off, handing her the cold cuts and rolls I had bought across the street, to make sandwiches. We hadn't eaten since breakfast.

After we ate, Milly took a T-shirt out of the bag. On it was an outline of the Dom with the words "SPEYER IST SPITZE."

"*Spitze,*" I said. "That means spire or something like that. Look in the dictionary.

"Yes," Milly replied. "Peak, extremity, top."

"That's it!" I interrupted. "It means 'Speyer is tops.'"

"*Speyer ist Spitze,*" Milly aped in her best German.

"Speyer is tops," I laughed.

* * * * *
13

We Are All Born Naked

W<small>E MISSED THE ENTRANCE</small> to the Autobahn and took the local road to Mannheim. "This must be the road I once bicycled from Speyer to Mannheim with my father," I remarked. I remembered that he was very kind when I got tired. Until this trip to Germany, it had always been one of my very few warm recollections of my father.

I approached Ludwigshafen with anticipation, recalling the huge old train station, my father's references to the chemical factory, the trolleys, the bridge to Mannheim, the beautiful parks. But I was in a rush to get to Aunt Helene, the traffic was atrocious, I misunderstood people's directions, rode around in circles, and hardly took notice of anything that I'd so much looked forward to seeing again. Yet when a big train station came into view I felt a tremendous thrill. I wanted to stop and see if it still had the high ceiling that Egon used to think touched heaven and maybe even God himself, if it still had the wooden benches, the cavernous blaring "train leaving on track" But I was in a frenzy and kept going.

"Relax," Milly said. "It's only five. We'll have at least two hours of daylight when we get to Schwegenheim."

We finally found the old-age home, on a quiet street across from a large park. Inside, from down a long corridor, Aunt Helene briskly came toward us. She had a strong, squarish, almost severe face with prominent blue eyes that did not smile—typically German? Her skin had few wrinkles; she could have been a woman in her seventies. It was hard to believe that she was eighty-six.

As we embraced, she apologized for the apron she was wearing over her dress. "I help out in the kitchen," she explained. "I was expecting you later, otherwise I would have waited for you in my room."

Aunt Helene's brisk manner struck me as not so much personality trait as that "German efficiency" I was so familiar with—a sort of crisp purposefulness that could be mistaken for coldness. But Aunt Helene's warmth came through. "Come, come into my home," she said, ushering us into a large sunny room furnished with an oriental carpet and with the walnut-veneer German-style furniture I knew so well—a breakfront displaying cut crystal, a matching round table covered with a lace cloth, and chairs that looked just like the ones my parents had. "This is my home," she said, waving her arm proudly, pointing out the efficiency kitchen and a large private bath.

"A pretty apartment, in a nice home," I commented.

"Yes," she said. "It is all my furniture."

"The same that is in a picture I have of you and Uncle Willie?"

"*Ja.*"

As we chatted, I noted the sharpness of her eighty-six-year-old mind. Was her unsmiling face a sign of age, a trait, or unhappiness? She spoke of her loneliness since my Uncle Willie had died years ago and now her worry about Lore's illness. "But the home is nice, the people are friendly, and I can maintain some independence here."

We talked of our families, present, and past. She spoke of my parents' visit in the 1960s, when Uncle Willie was still alive. And we spoke, inevitably, of the terrible war, of the relatives who were killed. "It is hard to think about it," she sighed. Uncle Willie was allowed to stay with her because she was not

Jewish, but six months before the war ended the Nazis took him away. "For the first month he worked in Berlin," she said. "For Eichmann."

My ears perked up, recalling my amazement at how Lore had spoken of this. "Yes," I said, "Lore told us. He cleaned stones?"

"Yes," she went on, now more softly, explaining, as Lore had, that he cleaned rubble after the bombings. "Officers left cigarettes for the Jewish workers."

I was stunned. These were Lore's exact words.

Then, with a hush in her voice, Aunt Helene said, "There is some good and some bad in all of us."

Word for word, she and Lore, like a script. No bitter tones. Nothing said about even a possibility that the cigarettes were given as crumbs of incentive to get more work out of the Jewish slaves! Or are they right? Is there some good in even the worst of human beings? And even if it is so, is that reason to forgive their terrible evil deeds?

"Willie was fortunate," Aunt Helene continued. "Along with a few thousand others who survived Teresienstadt. The S.S. were about to blow the camp up when the Russians liberated it."

We talked about how they resumed their lives after the war. I recalled the zither Uncle Willie sent Walt for his bar mitzvah in 1973. Aunt Helene reminded me that Uncle Willie died soon after that. "I converted to Judaism two years before he died," she said proudly.

"Really!" I said in surprise.

She told us that she still goes to synagogue once in a while and that Jews have been coming again to Mannheim, mostly from Eastern Europe.

When we took pictures, Milly got a smile out of Aunt Helene. We had to leave after less than an hour, but Aunt Helene told us how glad she was we'd come to see her. She walked us outside, pointing to the beautiful park across the street, where she often walks. But she felt lonely and hoped I would stay in touch. "I myself don't like to write," she warned. "Like your father," she added with a smile.

"Well, Aunt Helene, I like to write," I said. "And I'll send you the pictures."

* * * * *

As I turned into the village of Schwegenheim, I slowed to a snail's pace, every nerve and fiber in my body poised to find something familiar. Past the gas station I'd seen at a distance two days before, the little village street curved to the left, then to the right, and suddenly I saw it on a little blue marker on a building: "Bahnhofstrasse." My old railroad street! I turned in and gaped, speechless and openmouthed, from one side of the street to the other at the old houses, until I suddenly bellowed "The *Eckhaus*. There's the *Eckhaus!!*"

"Where, where? Milly asked, catching my excitement.

"The corner, the corner. The house on the corner there to the left."

"That's a regular house. Where is the egg house?" she asked.

"Not egg," I exclaimed, stopping the car." *Eck, Eck*—corner. *Eckhaus*—the corner house. Let's see the dictionary. Corner is *Ecke*. I remember it from the old pictures. My parents used to live in it. I don't know exactly when or how long. My grandparents' house was just a house or two down, on the same side."

I drove slowly on, my eyes glued to the left. Suddenly I stopped again, at a house with a store-front-type window at one end. Could it be? My grandparent's house had a store. But this seemed different. I could get out and ask. But I must see my woods before it gets dark.

I drove on, still looking to the left, hoping now for some trace of the Peppermint Train station. The only thing I saw was a large brick shed that was full of straw. Could that have been it? I didn't think so, but it could have been a railroad shed. In a few seconds, I saw the familiar fields and beyond them a most persistent memory of my early boyhood, the Schwegenheim woods.

Had I been walking, I would have sprung ahead to meet the embrace of those trees just as I had when I was a little boy. I sped the car to the edge of the woods, stopping at a small rest area with two log benches. "That wasn't there," I said. But the path into the woods was there. Though now paved, it looked just as it had in my faded memories.

I leapt out of the car. I felt almost dizzy as my eyes darted around. Looking down the path, I pictured my grandmother and Aunt Selma pushing a wooden cart, with me in it.

Is it really me, Edgar, standing here in 1983? It's hard to believe. Is it Egon? Is it a dream? Is it a culmination of fifty years of dreams—dreams that often depicted a little boy lost in the woods?

Milly was standing near the car, her head lowered. When I told her I needed to walk alone, she understood.

I strode down the path, almost soldier-like, eyes left, eyes right, eyes straight ahead. The trees and underbrush filled my nostrils with their warm summer fragrance. Far ahead was a break in the woods. Was that the route of the Peppermint Train? I yearned to see it. But it was nearing eight o'clock, and soon dusk would fall. I stopped. My eyes searched for a clearing, the clearing where I sat on a blanket with a basket of grapes while Oma, Mother and Aunt Selma scampered around collecting *Hutzele.*

My eyes scanned the ground for a trace of the *Hutzele.* Then something strange happened. Abruptly, the woods darkened. But not because of the long shadows cast by the lowering sun. The woods darkened from my gloomy thoughts. I found myself standing at attention, as if in fear. I saw that some of the trees were very old, dating back at least to my boyhood, but that many of the trees must be the offspring of those that had died. Suddenly the older trees turned into Nazis standing at attention, and a kaleidoscope of pictures shot through my brain: Germans with outstretched arms singing *"Deutschland, Deutschland über Alles,"* Hitler gesticulating, calling the Jews vermin, Nazis marching, smashing Jewish store windows, a young Nazi tough threatening to beat me up with his belt on the way to school, swastika flags flying, banners and voices demanding, *"Juden raus," "Juden verreckt."*

I felt dread. I was lost, trapped, alone in the woods, not allowed out. I saw myself on the train to Stuttgart, my mother whispering, "Shshsh, don't cough," worried that we wouldn't be allowed out of the country.

I shook myself, lifted one foot, then the other, and stood with my feet apart. "You bastards," I mumbled under my breath. Flailing my arms in rage, I began to walk back toward the car.

"You lousy bastards, you kicked me out of this lovely place, out of my woods, my Schwegenheim, my Speyer, my homeland." I stopped, clenched my fists, looked at the trees, walked on, pounded my fists into the air, then downward toward the ground, crying, "You bastards, what did I ever do to you?" I saw my grandfather in our kitchen in Speyer, confronting a German man who was denouncing him as a Jew. "What did I ever do to you?" Opa asked him.

My rage subsided, and the images turned to questions, the same old questions, but questions I had never before felt so keenly: How could civilized man do the things this nation did? How could an advanced, productive culture produce such horrors? What is it in the human condition that causes us to kill each other, even as now we are faced with technology that threatens not just the extinction of select millions but of the species itself? Will we ever find the answers? I wanted to think so. It was not enough to merely be angry.

As I returned to the car, my arms hung loosely at my sides. My eyes turned to the ground here and there looking for *Hutzele*, and my lungs breathed deeply the delicious aromas of trees and shrubs and mushrooms and wildflowers.

* * * * *

Back in Schwegenheim, I parked at the building I thought might have been the train station. As I took a picture and peered down the Bahnhofstrasse, an old woman came out of her yard across from where we stood. "My grandparents lived here over fifty years ago," I told her. "Their name was Walther. I am trying to find their house."

"Yes," she said. "I think it was up further."

I drove to the two-story structure with the store-front window. This time I noted a doorway next to the window, and other details. There was a wooden gate enclosing a yard to my left, next to that a brick barn-like structure with no windows fronting the street, and then the *Eckhaus*. The old pictures back home showed that a yard connected my parents' and grandparents' house, and I recalled the old photo of my mother standing in the doorway of the store, her hats in one window, my grandfather's groceries in the other. Yes this was the house, but it had been completely remodeled.

I started to take pictures from across the street. Then a middle-aged man appeared, puzzled about what we were looking for. When he heard my story, he rushed inside to get his mother-in-law.

She had thin hair, mostly white, parted in the center and combed into a bun, a pleasant ruddy face with puffed cheeks, a broad pug nose, some fuzz on the chin, and a strong neck on a robust body with arms that had done a good deal of physical work. A colorfully checkered, work-worn housecoat covered a rotund belly. To me she looked like a prototypical German peasant woman.

"Yes, what are you looking for?" she asked, through a kind, partly toothless mouth.

"My name is Stern. My grandparents used to live here."

She peered at me, her ruddy cheeks turned deep red, her broad nose widened, her thick eyebrows rose into her forehead, and her large pupils became saucers. "*Du bist der Egon!!*" she trumpeted loud enough for the whole neighborhood to hear, her robust arms spreading wide into the air and then swooping down around me.

"*Ach, der Egon . . . Egon Stern!*" she bellowed, stepping back to peer at me in happy disbelief, alternately clapping and clasping her large hands. "*Du bist der Egon!* Can I call you '*Du*'? I knew you so well when you were a small child."

"*Ja*," I replied, happily accepting the familiar personal pronoun.

"And Selma," she blared. "Selma. Your mother's sister. I went to school with her. Kapp was my name. Elise Kapp."

"Yes, my Aunt Selma; she is still living. My parents are both dead. But Selma is still alive."

"Oh, I knew your whole family so well. Your grandparents, Loui and Lina, they lived in that house there," she said, pointing across the street. "We were like one big family here," she continued, clapping her hands in cadence to each exclamation. "And your parents, that used to be their house on the corner, the *Eckhaus*."

"Yes, I recognized the *Eckhaus* right away. But my grandparents' house not so quickly."

"It's changed a lot," she said.

"I must go in to call my sister," Elise continued with unabated jubilance. "She knew your Aunt Selma too and the rest of your family. And we must get Hanna," she said, turning to her son-in-law. "And go get Mariele."

"Mariele!" I said with amazement. It was the only name I recognized so far. "She is still here!"

"Yes, yes, she is still here in Schwegenheim."

Elise went back inside, and while I went to photograph the *Eckhaus*, I noticed Elise's son-in-law walking from house to house, apparently in such a state of excitement that he stopped in the middle of the street not quite sure where to go next. "This is all very interesting to me," I told him, at a loss for better words.

He nodded, "Yes, I can really believe that. It is for me too."

Elise came back out and began talking animatedly to Milly. As I walked over, she looked at me again saying, "Egon, Egon Stern. I can hardly believe it. And this is your wife."

"Milly," I said, realizing that in the excitement I hadn't even introduced her.

"Milly," Elise repeated, shaking her hand warmly. "I knew your husband so well when he was a little boy. And his whole family I knew. Oh! Here comes Hanna.

"Hanna, would you believe who this is that came to see us. This is, Egon, Loui and Lina's grandson, Selma's nephew."

Hanna was a short, white-haired woman with a sort of universal kind-grandmother appearance. Her head cocked back somewhat bashfully, as she peered up at me from behind white-framed glasses and then edged over for a shy but warm handshake.

Sufficiently recovered from my dumbfoundedness at meeting all these people from my early childhood, of whom I had no recollection, I tried to concentrate on understanding Elise's rapid chatter in the Pfalz dialect. I started to respond in that same familiar dialect and then laughed, "*Joh. Ich konn noch Pfälzerisch Deutsch spreche.*"

I pointed at my grandparents' house. "There was a double

store-window where that one modern window is now, right? With a door between the two windows?"

Elise confirmed it, told more about the house and started telling anecdotes about my grandparents. Much of it I couldn't understand, but I nodded anyhow. Hanna continued to gape at me in fascination, with a remarkable steady smile, nodding rhythmically to Elise's stories. Then she excused herself and soon returned with a photo album. At that moment Elise looked up the block and shouted, "Here comes Mariele!" and I saw a gray-haired woman furiously pedaling her bicycle toward us. As she screeched to a halt, Elise bellowed *"Mariele, der Egon ist hier."*

Mariele held her bicycle as if to steady herself, her head cocked somewhat backward, and gazed at me blinking her eyes in amazement as if she was seeing an apparition.

She opened her mouth, half declaring and half asking, *"Des is der Egon!?"*

"Yes, I am Egon. Can you believe it?"

"Egon," she said, incredulously.

"Mariele," I said, shaking hands and gawking in amazement into her eyes, not daring to embrace, even though an almost brotherly feeling swept over me. Although I had no actual memory of her, I said instinctively, "Mariele, I know you well."

She continued to stare at me with her head slightly back, her eyes still squinting for comprehension, her chin seeming to hold up her astonished set cheeks and taut lips. She continued to hold on to her bike as if for security, while I just as incredulously stared back at her. Here was Mariele, who I remembered only from my family's occasional reminiscences after we left Germany. Here was the Mariele whose aged face now brought back to mind an old photo in which as a teen-age girl she was a bridesmaid in Aunt Selma's wedding.

"And this is his wife, Milly," Elise said, breaking the silence.

As they shook hands, Mariele asked if she was German-born too.

"American," Milly said.

"I was close to you and your family," Mariele told me. "I worked with your mother, even lived with you for a while in Speyer."

Hanna continued to nod and smile shyly but now edged closer, opening the album and telling of a photo. "Here is your Oma and Opa," she pointed, then turned the pages to show a photo of Aunt Selma holding me when I was a few months old. It was a touching photo that I'd never seen before. Oh, if I could only find the right German phrases to express my feeling, I thought, coming up only with *"Sehr interessant"* but nodding vigorously.

How fantastic this is, I thought to myself. I suddenly appear here after fifty years and some of these people held on to my family pictures. Who would keep photos of us if they believed the vile things Hitler said about us? My grandparents were on her first page!

I remarked about the yard in which the pictures were taken, noting the cobblestones, the shrubbery in the background.

"That was your yard and garden," they all sang out.

"And we used to have a goat there, they tell me," I said.

"Ja, Ja," they cried, Mariele now clapping her hands, adding that my grandparents also had chickens and geese in the yard.

"They used to slaughter them themselves," Elise cried out, laughing.

A vision of my grandfather slashing a goose's neck again flashed through my mind, the animal continuing to dance wildly around the yard without a head.

A couple from the house next to my grandparents' came over. The man extended a hearty handshake introducing himself and his wife as Otto and Gisela Galle. "We noticed a couple in a red Opel a while ago," he said. "I figured they must be looking for something."

"I knew your family," Gisela said, shaking hands.

More people gathered around us, and as Elise went on about my family, especially about Selma, Otto took my hand again and said "How nice it is that you came back to visit the village where you spent your childhood. His face was intense and sincere, and he held on to my hand, *"Mein Dorf ist immer mein Dorf* (One's village is forever one's village)."

Elise said that my grandparents' house used to be a gathering point for all the neighbors. Otto explained that he didn't come to Schwegenheim until 1941 and therefore didn't know my family, but he knew what the old house looked like. A hayloft used to cover part of the house, and it was converted to a full second story. And yes, there used to be two store-front windows.

Suddenly Elise again trumpeted a cheer as another gray-haired woman came pedaling on her bicycle toward us: "Here comes my sister Emma, who knew Loui and Lina and Selma, and your parents." Emma jumped off her bike, shrieked "Egon, Egon," wrapped her arms around me, and kissed me, starting to chatter about how well she knew us all, citing every name, how she went to school with Selma. Now everybody seemed to be talking at once, almost competing to ask me questions and to tell their reminiscences. Mariele asked about my mother's brother Leon. I told her he died shortly after he came to America. Someone mentioned Uncle Fish. "Oh yes, Uncle Fish," I said. Someone else shouted, "He used to live up the street." Indeed it was the house I recalled, a triangular one that jutted out into the street. "He was a big, fat, friendly man," I said, everyone laughingly agreeing.

I mentioned the Loebs. "They lived in *Gommershe*," Mariele said. "*Ja*, Gommershe, Gommersheim," I repeated. I told them about my last ride on the *Pfefferminzzug* to visit the Loebs. Everybody hushed, listening. Otto then said the train doesn't run any more; it was abandoned in 1956. "But the station still stands," someone else said. The subject changed as everybody started talking again, and I was to end my pilgrimage without knowing more about my Peppermint Train.

"I went to school with Selma," Elise said to Emma. "I did too," someone else said. "And we had so much fun playing together," they both laughed, "Selma was always so much fun." "Selma was here in Schwegenheim in the 1960s," I heard someone say. "She didn't stay long," someone else said.

"And Loui and Lina," Elise continued, "were so good to everybody. They used to bring matzos when they had their Passover, and we used to go over to eat their matzo ball soup. How we used to love it." Emma told of the times when she and her sister would arrive home from school and couldn't find a bit of food in their own house. "We went over to Loui and Lina who fed us. What good people they were. Always shared with everybody. And what good people the other *'Judde'* were." I flinched inwardly at the word *Judde*, wondering, isn't this a pejorative for *Juden*, for Jews? Or is it dialect? Or just a diminutive?

Elise went on about how friendly she was with the other Jews in the village, where the synagogue used to be, and other things my slow German couldn't keep up with. But I heard one woman proudly tell the crowd that during the Hitler years she never followed the dictum to stay away from the Jews. "I was told personally that if I continued to fraternize, the Gestapo would get me too. But I defied them by daring them to get me." Mariele looked at me with her quiet eyes and said, "I stayed with your family till the end. I used to go to synagogue with you, even till the very last." I nodded, my eyes lighting up, amazed at my total lack of memory for that. Was it really so? Why didn't I have any recollection of it? I remembered so much else! And yet, as soon as I saw Mariele today there was something eerily familiar about her.

Someone said something about the *Eckhaus*, and my eyes turned toward it. Just then a somewhat stooped, frail-looking man in a brown suit, a buttoned-up sport shirt, and a straw hat, walked slowly toward us. He looked to be in his eighties. "Here comes Lehmen," someone said. As he joined the group, someone told him who I was, but he must have already known, for he immediately took me by the arm, lightly with thin, aged fingers. His deep blue eyes penetrated mine as he slowly said, in a thin quavering voice that reflected both his advanced years and his excitement: *"Lehmen . . . Lehmen, ist mein Namen."* Then he squeezed my arm and with almost tearful eyes continued, *"Ich . . . habe . . . von Ihren Eltern . . . das Eckhaus . . . gekauft."*

He had bought my parents' corner house! He pulled at my sleeve and pointing toward the house continued with slow quivering precision: *"Am 22 Dezember 1928."* "He still lives there," I heard someone say.

What an incredible thing, to meet the person who fifty-five years ago bought that *Eckhaus* from my parents. I didn't even know that my parents had actually owned the house!

Tuning in again to the dozen or more people now crowded around us, I heard Elise bellow a story about my grandfather.

The village was having a celebration, and they were roasting a pig in her yard. My grandfather had helped to slaughter the pig, and during the festival he came over. "He took a taste of the meat," Elise laughed, "when suddenly Lina appeared, and oh how she scolded him!" "Loui and Lina kept kosher," Mariele explained to the assemblage.

Otto, who had disappeared for a moment, returned with the couple who now occupied my grandparents' house. The husband opened a manila envelope and showed me a page from a photo album with two pictures of his house. "Before and after the reconstruction," he said. Would you like to photograph these pictures?" "It's too dark now," someone said. "Do you have a flash?" Otto asked, as I started to pull it out of my bag. I laid the sheet on the sidewalk and photographed it. "Take another one, just in case," Otto insisted.

More and more, I felt Otto's intense interest and sincerity.

"These pictures are very meaningful to me," I said.

"Yes. And you must show them to your Aunt Selma," Otto urged. "And now why doesn't everyone come into our house and have some wine," he added. "We'll toast your return to the village, and Selma."

I looked at my watch. It was 9:30, and night was falling. I still want to see Gommersheim, I explained, and we have to get up early the next morning for our return flight.

Otto left again, telling us not to leave until he returned. We chatted about how much we enjoyed our visit here, and Mariele said that in 1985 there would be a big celebration in Schwegenheim—the village's one-thousandth anniversary. Maybe I could come back for it.

Otto returned, handing me two bottles of wine. "This is for you, and for Aunt Selma who I heard so much about tonight."

"And tell her about me," Gisela said. "My maiden name was Dickgiesen."

"Yes," Otto said, "Dickgiesen. They were my wife's parents. And when you come back here, as we hope you will, you can stay with us, any time. Come back for the anniversary.

"Anyone can stay at our place," Otto continued, amidst the good-byes. "My parents taught me well. They persistently lived by the rule that it doesn't matter who anyone is. They taught me a proverb: 'In the womb there is no textile industry.' Do you know what that means?"

When I hesitated, he added, "We are all born naked."

The old man took my hand again. "I bought your parents' house, on the 22 of December 1928. Remember, Lehmen. Tell Selma."

As I started to leave, I looked at Mariele, and hesitated. Then I went over to kiss her. Elise and Emma giggled warmly, "Yes. Mariele was the closest."

Otto walked us to our car, giving us his address, repeating that we should come back for Schwegenheim's anniversary and stay with him. "One's village is forever one's village."

As we drove away, everyone waved, and chanted, in German and in English: "*Aufwiedersehen*, good-bye."

Though weary, and very hungry, I felt a wonderful warmth but also the omnipresent underlying sadness.

"Such warm human beings," Milly said. "This is the first time I felt fully comfortable in Germany."

It was dark when we entered Gommersheim, and as I vainly searched in the blackness for the Loeb house I realized that Gommersheim represented not only my last ride on the Peppermint Train but the end of my German-Jewish boyhood, and the end to all those neighborly relationships that I had rediscovered on this trip.

* * * * *

The next morning, at the Frankfurt airport, I saw a rack of T-shirts. Imprinted on them was the emblem of Germany—an eagle—and the word "Deutschland." I stared at the shirts for a moment and then whispered to Milly, "Look, those T-shirts. I could never have anybody in my family wear one of them."

* * * * *

As the plane left the ground, I thought I would never be able to see Germany again, and I felt sad about leaving. In the ensuing hours, I thought of the places I did not get to see—the Messplatz, Gommersheim, Kaiserslautern, Dolgesheim, Seeheim. Warm moments from the trip kept returning to mind, as well as agitating questions: One's village is forever one's village . . .

Come back for the 1000th anniversary . . . Mariele was the closest . . . Such warm human beings in Schwegenheim . . . "I defied them by daring them to get me . . ." But what did some of the others do to the Jews? . . . *Juden raus* . . . I was kicked out . . . What causes us to kill each other? Is there some good in even the worst? We are all born naked. . . .

* * * * *
14

Looking for Redemption

MILLY'S BROTHER NORMAN, a Judaic studies scholar, had been very interested in my trip to Germany. He and his wife, Geri, sat spellbound as I recounted my experiences with a dramatic slide show.

"What did you feel when you shook hands with your former playmate?" Norman asked.

"When I shook hands, when I sat in his house, everything was overshadowed by the feeling of reunion. But I felt ambivalent afterward," I continued, "wondering what they did to the Jews."

"And who knows what went through *their* minds, and through some of the others' you met, or what they talked about after they saw you?" Norman said. "Here you suddenly show up in their homes fifty years later. They might have thought, 'Why do you have to come back to remind me?'"

"With Konrad and Klaus I began to feel that Germans were human beings," Milly said. "Before that I walked around with my own images, my own anxiety, and this was the first time I could see a German as a human being. They were both very nice. And those people in Schwegenheim were so affectionate."

"It reminds me of something I read," said Norman. "'The banality of evil,' Arendt called it. You go back to Germany expecting to see monsters; in fact you almost want to meet somebody that will justify your rage. But then you come up against doggone ordinary human beings."

"Like human beings anywhere, acting according to the dictates of their environment—both the good and the evil," I said. "Are the four of us here immune to doing evil?"

"Vietnam was no picnic," Geri observed. "And Jews have committed atrocities."

"But does all that excuse the Holocaust?" I said. "That's what I'm struggling with. I can't shake the fact that it was damned Germans who did it; and they kicked me out!"

"It's obvious how you're wrestling obsessively with these things," Geri said. "Do you think you'll ever make peace with your feelings, Ed?"

"Peace?!" I blurted out. "I wonder if a survivor can ever make peace! And though I'm not a survivor, I don't know if I can. I lived a comfortable life while others went through hell, even had fun on a boat coming to America. When I was a teenager during the war I don't think I even thought about what was going on over there. And now I can't stop thinking about it."

"What I meant," Geri said, "is a kind of settlement with your feelings or some answers to your questions."

"Well, I ripped my name tag off in Trier and if I hadn't crumpled it I probably would have stuck it back on. And I asked for my boyhood fairy-tale book in the store. And I raised hell in the woods. Maybe those kinds of things were little bits of settlement with my feelings."

In the weeks that followed, as I refocused my earliest memories, I came to realize that the little Peppermint Train was at the center of the warmest recollections of my German childhood. From time to time during the forty-seven years since I had left the train behind, it had knocked on the prison walls behind which my brain had placed it and made me smile. During some of those moments, I wanted to pick up a pencil and write a little story about it. But I never did—until now. And as I wrote, I began to cry. And then I knew that those tears about the Peppermint Train came from losing a wonderful childhood. And from the thought that while my central memory was a charming little Peppermint Train, a central memory for many others was a train to the death camps. And the tears were for those whose memories perished there.

Indeed, my memories and my anger unleashed a passion for finding out everything about my early life, for getting to know my relatives again—both the living and the dead—for understanding what had happened, and for an understanding of myself and my place in this saga.

In 1936 after I arrived in America, the Alabama relatives who had just changed my name from Egon to Edgar asked, "Why is he so quiet?" At that time, I did not know. After my 1983 trip, I knew: In 1936 I had pushed parts of me back. In 1983 I let them out again. And although I agonized about my unsettled feelings and questions, I realized that something inside me had changed. The trip had done a great deal for me. Milly observed that I was more relaxed than in the twenty-six years she had known me.

Something time-frozen within me had begun to thaw.

* * * * *

Some days, Otto's words haunted me: "You must come back for the 1000-year Schwegenheim celebration in 1985." The places I missed seeing kept coming back to mind—Kaiserslautern, Dolgesheim, Seeheim; the Messplatz; the Loeb house.

When I wrote to the people I met in Speyer and Schwegenheim, it was with an undertone of doubt: is it right to reestablish relationships with those who may have forsaken us or worse? But every time a letter came from Germany, I couldn't wait to open it. When Otto sent pictures of the Peppermint Train I was thrilled, when Konrad sent a diagram of my apartment on Markusweg I was so proud of having recalled it perfectly. When Klaus sent a huge "Speyer Gestern" (Speyer Yesteryear) calendar with a 1914 photo of the Postplatz on the cover I nearly did a jig. As I leafed through it, I jumped up exclaiming "Oh my God, here is the old pontoon bridge. With the railroad tracks!" And when I heard from Mariele and Elise, and from the mayors of Speyer and Schwegenheim whom I had written for information, I was happy.

It was Otto who became my regular correspondent. He'd been intensely interested in us in Schwegenheim and now his letters were always sincere and prompt, and he continually urged me to return for the anniversary.

Wouldn't it be interesting to be in my little village for its millennial celebration, I thought wistfully, and spend more time with those people to learn more about my family history. I even imagined talking more directly with Konrad and Klaus about their feelings during the war and their experiences with the Nazis. No, I wouldn't ask. What good would the facts do even if they remembered and gave them to me? Those facts wouldn't help me resolve the issues I'm trying to resolve. On the other hand, if they had tormented or killed Jews, I'd have to close the book on them. Is that why I'd want to know? Or not want to know?

* * * * *

"I can't figure out why I want to go back again," I told Norman. "I know about the impulse of going back to one's roots, but to a place which kicked you out and killed your relatives?"

"You left there just at an age when a person puts himself together, forms a full identity with himself and his world," Norman said. "And you don't throw off those things, the identifications, the patriotism."

The words "identifications, patriotism" made my face turn red, then hot, reminding me of something terribly embarrassing that had bothered me for years. "We're alone," I started. "I want to tell you something that I've never said to anyone before. My darkest secret. If I'd told this to anyone else I'd feel they'd think me nuts. Over the years I've experienced this frightful thing. But it just comes to me, into my head: The tune and works of the old German national anthem, *Deutschland, Deutschland über Alles.*"

"A good example of the horrible ambivalence," Norman said. "Identifying with the persecutors. And for you it wasn't even so much that. You were only a kid. You didn't know what the song really meant, any more than a young kid knows what the 'Star Spangled Banner' really means, or the 'Hatikvah.'"

I fell silent, relieved that something oppressive had been

lifted from my mind. Then I told Norman about the way I rushed from one place to the other on the trip, meeting people, seeing the past.

"You had denied a whole span of time—nine years of it," Norman observed. "You went on the trip because you were ready to fill in that time period, and miraculously people came from all over the place and filled it in for you."

What Norman said was true. Despite all the therapy I'd had, that childhood was hardly part of my consciousness. "Something had been torn away from me," I said, "and I was trying to reconnect it, reclaim it."

"And people who are persecuted," Norman said, "often conclude that they did something wrong."

Yes, I thought, maybe I went back to hear that Egon didn't do anything wrong, that it wasn't his fault.

"It's like looking for redemption," Norman continued. "And you don't get that so much by reading books and talking about it. You feel redeemed just seeing those people—nothing specific even needs to be said."

And for the next few months I wondered—can I go back again?

* * * * *

When Aunt Selma went back to Germany in the 1960s, she'd visited Schwegenheim but neither Speyer nor Kaiserslautern. It would have been too painful for her, she told me.

Aunt Selma's health had improved after a bypass operation, and she was attentive when I showed her the slides and the huge new photo album into which I had organized all of the old family pictures. Though her mind wandered, there was a hint of happy recognition of some of her old friends from Schwegenheim.

Two of her aged German-Jewish friends watched the slides with her, and I asked them if they had ever been back, or if they would ever go back.

"No!" Betty said. She'd been in Switzerland a few years ago, just minutes from the border, but would not enter Germany. Before the war she had reached safety in England, she explained, but her father was killed in a concentration camp.

"Neverrr," seventy-five-year-old Minnie said, in her Lithuanian accent.

"Why?" I asked.

"Vy?' You should ask!" she exclaimed, her shoulders rising. "I tell you vy. To set foot on German soil vood be like steppink on Jewish blood."

I felt my face turn crimson, and my eyelids flutter, as I saw the main street of Speyer. It was red.

"No, neverrr," she added. "I vood be afraid of steppink on the bones of my people."

Something I had read the day before sprung to life: While digging a construction site somewhere in Germany, workers came across hundreds of human bones.

* * * * *

Now that my emotions had surfaced, I felt terribly ignorant about the Holocaust, despite my previous readings. And my guilt at how little interest I'd shown in the Holocaust as a youngster continued to grow. I pressed myself to be more forgiving of this. Wasn't I, like other ordinary teenagers and young adults, just trying to get on with life?

I also felt sorry for how harshly I had judged my father. Perhaps he was smarter than I'd ever realized. I had often thought him paranoid because he had so little trust for people. But he had reason to be mistrustful, losing to the Nazis everything he had worked so hard for. I needed to find out more about my father, too.

My research became an obsession. Maybe it was a response to my guilt feelings, maybe a search for redemption. I sought not only more intellectual knowledge but also information about my relatives and former friends like Rabbi Marx.

I wrote to Holocaust resource centers, traveled to New York to search the archives of German Jewry at the Leo Baeck Institute. I visited relatives I hadn't seen in decades: my aged cousins in New Rochelle, Robert and Martha from Dolgesheim; Lillian and Hugo from Seeheim; Jeanette Loeb; my cousin Samuel Schloss in Alabama, the son of Aunt Amelia who had brought us to America. I wrote to my "uncle" David in France. But I was doing more than accumulating information.

The frantic activity served as catharsis, as a way of reconnecting with my family, and as a vehicle for deciding whether to go back in 1985.

I read that after the war, Albert Einstein received many invitations to return. He felt that as a self-respecting Jew he could not possibly be associated in an official way with any German institution. "The crime of the Germans is truly the most abominable ever to be recorded in the history of so-called civilized nations," he said. Others stated that they could not return because they'd be sitting next to murderers.

Yet Leo Baeck, the prewar spiritual leader of the German Jews, was in 1948 one of the first prominent Jews to make a return trip. While acknowledging there could be no resumption of the "spiritual relationship" between Jews and Germans, Baeck believed that it was his responsibility to nurture some kind of relationship. He also came to realize that the Germans had to look deep into their souls to understand why they had adopted Nazism.

I reasoned that if Baeck went back, so could I. My parents went back too, and I now regretted never having found out how they felt when they saw the homeland. But I know they didn't visit Speyer or Schwegenheim, and that in itself says something. I think they went to Germany primarily, if not entirely, to visit my father's relatives in Mannheim as a side trip while vacationing in Switzerland.

As I talked to my relatives, I asked each of them how they felt about going back. When Ria, a distant cousin who was born in Mannheim, came to see the slides, we talked about her concentration camp experiences. "No," she said tentatively when I asked if she'd ever visit Germany. "There's many other places I'd rather go to. But if I ever went near the country, I might want to see Mannheim again. Of that I have fond memories."

Cousin Robert seemed strained when I asked him to talk about Germany. He didn't even show any enthusiasm for his native village of Dolgesheim. But he remembered "just like it was yesterday" when Germany's President Hindenburg made Hitler chancellor. "Hindenburg thought it would be for only a short time," Robert laughed sarcastically.

"I remember vividly what I ran into in those years," he

continued. "I lived in Mannheim and took extensive business trips through Bavaria. When I got home I told people how hard it was for a Jew to get a room, and about all the Nazi parades and anti-Jewish posters. So I told my friends and relatives, 'Listen, it's very bad. We've got to do something.' But they shushed me and said, 'Forget it, it will go away.'" Robert's voice rasped and his veins bulged from his temples: "The Jewish people thought that by being nice everything would be all right! Even the German people, and many of the politicians thought so!"

I asked if they'd ever been back to Germany.

"No," said his wife, Martha, emphatically. "That's all in the past. Forgotten."

"You could pay me a million dollars and I wouldn't go!" Robert said.

When I visited Lillian and Hugo, we recalled how Hugo hated New York City when they came to America in 1937. He had soon bought a house in New Rochelle and used to kid us about our staying in the concrete jungle. I'd always agree with him, and loved visiting them in "the country."

I plied them with questions about Seeheim. They told me it was a little town in the foothills of the Odenwald, a mountain range south of Frankfurt. Hugo had a butcher shop in their house, and Lillian used to board summer vacationers.

One photo in my album showed Lillian standing beside a horse and buggy at a yellowish-brick house. I thought it was their house in Seeheim.

"No, that was my parents' house in Dolgesheim," Lillian said.

"Oh, now I understand why the picture shows me with Uncle Moses in the buggy. I must have been not much over a year old." I recounted my delightful memory of Uncle Moses picking us up at the little train station with the horse and buggy, then driving us up a thrilling steep hill to the house. "The first house on the left as you entered Dolgesheim, correct?"

"Yes, yes," they chanted. "The train station was in Hillesheim."

"Was it a big train," I asked, "or one of those little ones?"

"A little local railroad," Hugo said. "I think you used to take the train from Speyer to Ludwigshafen, then a train to Worms, and from there the little train to Dolgesheim."

"Was it far from Seeheim?" I asked.

"It was then," they said. "Now you can drive there in less than an hour."

When I asked what happened to them under the Nazis, Hugo said that as early as 1933 the Nazis had hidden a camera in a house aross the street and photographed customers patronizing his store. Many customers came anyhow, after dark, but eventually more and more had to stop.

"It wasn't easy to get the immigration papers," Lillian said. "You know, I was hard of hearing. And the Americans were strict. I don't know what we would have done without Amelia Schloss and and Jeanette Loeb."

"And even after we got the papers," Hugo said, "the Nazis took them back three times."

"The morning we finally left," Lillian added, "Nazis stood in front of our house and sang *'Wenn Judenblut vom Messer spritzt dann gehts nochmal so gut.'*" "'When Jewish blood spurts from the knife, then all goes twice as well,'" Hugo translated. "Yes, that's what the bastards sang," Hugo said.

"Were any of your relatives killed?" I asked.

"An uncle and a nephew," Lillian said.

"My father was over seventy," Hugo said, his voice now at a high pitch, his aged face straining. "My father told me, 'You don't have to go to America. The Nazis won't last.' He stayed, and they killed him."

But when Hugo and Lillian showed me their postwar picture book of Seeheim, I noted how fond they still were of their hometown. "Yes," they said, "it was a pretty little town, peaceful mountains all around," and Hugo wistfully recalled their house at "3 Darmstadterstrasse—near the pretty old *Rathaus*, the town hall."

I told them of my memory about the big swimming pool in Seeheim.

"That was in Jugenheim, the next village," Hugo said.

Lillian was amazed that I remembered when she and my mother took me to the pool, despite the sign about Jews not being allowed. "Yes," she sighed, "at that time they weren't bothering children yet."

"Did you ever go back to visit?" I asked.

"Yes, but I couldn't stay long," Hugo said, tears forming in his eyes. "I went out to walk the street before six in the morning so I wouldn't have to look at the Germans. And so they wouldn't see me cry."

Well, I said to myself, others who went back share some of my feelings. Some of them also pine for their hometowns, despite what happened. But although I felt I wanted to return, whenever I thought about it there was always a bit of doubt, sadness or anger. If it didn't come out immediately, it haunted me later, and it entered into my dreams. One night I dreamt that the mayor of Schwegenheim had invited me back for a visit. I accepted, on condition that I be allowed to make a speech on human rights. He agreed, and I went.

* * * * *

The last time I had seen Jeanette Loeb—cousin to Uncle Julius of Gommersheim—was at my mother's funeral in 1972. After my father's funeral in 1979, Jeanette called to chide me for forgetting to invite her. "I liked your folks," she reminded me. "Remember, Edgar, I helped you to get to America."

Now, when I visited her, her directness, her strong but pleasant voice, and her liking for me and my family came through again. Kurt, her husband, had a deep gentle voice with a light German accent.

I was eager to know more about Jeanette's part in our coming to America. "Yes, Sam Schloss was an extremely wealthy man," she told me. "A multimillionaire. His father, a German immigrant, started a wholesale grocery company in Montgomery." Amelia Schloss was my Oma's sister's daughter, Jeanette reminded me. When Amelia wanted to send for us, she wrote to Jeanette in New York. "I'd been a German major in college, and Amelia didn't know a word of German."

"Oh, but I found very old letters from Amelia, as far back as the 1920s, and they were in German," I told her.

"No, Edgar," Jeanette said. "Other people in Montgomery

wrote those letters for her. Amelia couldn't even say hello in German. That's why she asked me to make the final arrangements with your family. And Edgar, I'll never forget the day when I picked you folks up from the boat. It was impossibly hot."

"The hottest day in New York history!" I interrupted.

"Yes, impossibly hot, Edgar. And your mother was so sick. She had a warm dress on, with long sleeves. I felt so sorry for her. And for all of you."

I asked if my memory was right, about the apartment on 103d Street, near the elevated train. Of course, I didn't mention the bedbugs. But she must have known, since I sensed her embarrassment. "Well, you know Edgar, the apartment was cheap," she said, quickly. "Amelia had sent me seventy-five dollars for you. And I had no idea of what you could afford."

Amelia and Jeanette also helped my father's brother Oscar and his wife to emigrate and all the relatives from Gommersheim. Jeanette's own father was born in Gommersheim and came to America in 1886, she explained. In 1928 she made a visit to the village. She remembered vividly her embarrassment about a gift she wanted to bring to her relatives. People here told her that my grandparents had "everything" in their store. "And so here I come from New York, picturing a department store like Macy's! And then I saw that tiny old place on the Bahnhofstrasse. I'll never forget it."

I was curious to know if she rode the little train, and what it looked like.

"All I can remember was the stink," she said.

"Stink?" I asked.

"Garlic," she said.

"No peppermint?"

"Edgar," she laughed, "if there was peppermint on that train I couldn't smell it. It smelled so bad from garlic I had to cough."

Jeanette's husband, Kurt, who was raised in a village near Gommersheim, explained that the train usually carried lots of peppermint but that garlic was also a local crop.

"It's lucky they didn't call it the garlic train," I said.

Kurt also remembered the little train warmly and drew me a sketch of it. Yes, he replied to my question, it had a small coal-burning engine which regularly emitted sooty smoke that invaded passenger's eyes and noses.

"Jeannette," I asked, "what did you know about the anti-Semitism in Germany during the thirties?"

"We heard from the family that it was bad there for a long time," she said. "But there was anti-Semitism in America too and so we didn't take those reports from Germany too seriously at first."

Kurt told a story about his best boyhood friend. "One Friday night my twelve-year-old friend was at my house for dinner—a Sabbath dinner—and he says to me, *"Kurt, der Jude ist der Hass der Völker."*

"That means something like 'Jew hatred is an inborn thing?'" I asked.

"More like, 'Everybody hates the Jews,'" Kurt explained, his face turning crimson. "And let me tell you, Edgar, that remark really stuck under my skin! And that boy later became a minister. And a big Nazi!" No, Kurt concluded, he would never go back to Germany.

* * * * *

Listening to other people's experiences and feelings only added to my confusion about going back to Germany again. At the same time, I intensified my research.

At the Leo Baeck Institute I came upon a list of Jews who were rounded up by the Nazis—Jews from Speyer, from Schwegenheim, from Gommersheim. My chest tightened. I searched for Rabbi Marx. I couldn't find him. Suddenly I saw the name "Boetigheimer, Lisolette." That was Lilo! She was the only other third grader in our Hebrew school class. We were playmates, too. Our families always joked that we'd be married some day.

I looked again, to make sure. Yes! Her birthdate is listed as April 27, 1927—the same age as I. It said that she and her family went to Johannesburg, South Africa. Of course! I remember my mother mentioning that some time after we came to America. I must try to trace Lilo.

I read on. Suddenly I saw the name "Walther, Ernest." A relative of my grandfather! He was listed as *"verschollen"*—

missing, presumed dead. A euphemism, of course, for "murdered."

I pressed on to find my rabbi and teacher. But there was no mention of him in this book.

When I finally found "Marx, Sigmund" in another book, I slapped both hands on the table. Yes, his first name was Sigmund—Sigmund Marx, who brought me the chocolate cake for Hanukkah. He had emigrated to Switzerland, was returned to Speyer; his disposition: *Verschollen.*"

Almost in tears, I walked down the hall to relieve tension, and uttered choking, halting words to the sympathetic librarian about what I'd found. Then, as I walked back to my book, I realized I had known for a long time that Lehrer Marx was dead. I had been trying to bring him back to life—trying to make a reconnection!

A few pages further on, my breath almost stopped. My Speyer synagogue! I could hardly stand it and almost closed the book. When I tried to look away, I literally felt my aching heart hold my eyes to the page. There was the doorway, where my father sat that day selling tickets to the Zionist movie. I turned the page. Oh God! Here is the inside of my synagogue, the wooden pews. I saw myself on the bima, singing "En Kelohenu."

Then I remembered sitting in the pews, trying desperately to keep from turning around to look at the two uniformed Germans watching us from the back row. Finally, during a prayer in which we had to turn toward the back of the synagogue, I saw them. They sat politely, but they were smirking.

I saw another scene. Maybe it happened the same day. The doors of the synagogue burst open. I heard shouts, *"Raus, raus. Raus Judde!"* People froze. Rabbi Marx stopped the prayers. He told us to leave, quietly. I saw anxiety-ridden faces. I heard my father tell my grandmother to take me home. I felt her tight grip on my hands as we rushed past the hollering Nazis.

When I opened the book to the next page, my synagogue was aflame in the night. I stared for a long time at the flames and at the words, "Kristallnacht, 9–10 November 1938."

I shut the book and left.

When I got into my car, I burst into tears. I had thought I was all cried out in Speyer. Too upset to drive, I walked the streets, and went to dinner. It was dark by the time I entered the New Jersey Turnpike. And in the privacy of the darkness, encouraged by the movement of the speeding car, my emotions boiled over.

Over the years, I had sat for endless hours doing various kinds of research, but no discoveries had ever made me jump like this with joy and with horror and rage. I am engaged in the discovery of my own life, I said to myself, my childhood, my hopes, my dreams, my connections. I'm catching up, getting to know parts of myself that I hadn't realized were there, and I'm filled with emotions that I've never expressed. Finally, I am mourning, for Lehrer Marx, for my synagogue, for all the things my relatives went through and all the people they lost. And for the first time I think I understand why many Jews won't set foot on German soil.

As I passed Newark Airport, the roar of planes sent my rage flying. "This is the world the way it is!" I shouted with a high-pitched sarcasm into my tape recorder. "Take off. Higher and higher, civilization goes. Then crash! The Holocaust. And then the next crash. More killings. And on and on it goes. Humanity, onward, upward, and backward. Progress? Shit! We haven't really learned a lesson. Have the Germans? And even if they have, there are other groups who would be pleased to have the Jews go up in smoke. And look what's happening to others, like in South Africa, like. . . ."

My rage turned to guilt. "I have a good life, in my home in suburbia. I escaped the terrors, the horrors. But I feel shame, too. Shame, oddly, for those who foolishly, magically thought that things would get better and therefore stayed until it was too late. Like Rabbi Marx. For the millions who didn't lift a finger to fight the Nazi bastards. Holy smokes! I'm now talking like those who accuse the Jews of not defending themselves. What would I have done?!"

Somebody was tailgating me, blinking his lights, though it was obvious I couldn't move over. "Stupid idiot!!" I shrieked. Then, when I moved over and he passed, I moved behind him, blinked my lights and shouted, "Wrap yourself around a pole!"

Stunned by my own violent impulses, I pulled into a service station and parked in a dark spot way back in the lot, continuing for a long time to think about love, hate, power, selfishness, rationality. I needed to find more answers. I had to go back to Germany!

Grandparents' house in Schwegenheim about 1925; groceries in one window, hats in the other. *Left to right:* Uncle Leon, grandfather, Mariele.

The *Eckhaus*, Egon's parents' house.

Garden of house in Schwegenheim. *Left to right:* Emma, Aunt Selma, Mariele, Egon.

Egon and his "Uncle" Moses' son Robert in Dolgesheim, 1928.

Left, Egon and his mother in Speyer in 1929.
Bottom left, Egon with Lore and his maternal grandmother. *Bottom right*, Egon with Lore and their paternal grandmother.

Egon with his grandfather Ludwig Walther.

Egon with Aunt Selma near Kaiserslautern.

Two views of Aunt Selma and Uncle Eugene's store in Kaiserslautern.

Speyer, 1936. *Left to right:* Egon, Cousin Gerd, Oma, and Opa (maternal grandparents).

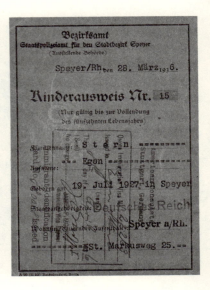

Egon's passport, 1936.

First family picture in America, July 1936. *Standing, left to right:* Uncle Eugene, Aunt Selma, Egon's father. *Seated, left to right:* Cousin Gerd, Egon's mother, Egon.

Egon and his parents in Speyer.

Anna Stern Krämer (Otto Stern's sister) and her children. *Left to right:* Lydia (died in Auschwitz), Gertrude (escaped to Sweden), and Anna (died in Auschwitz).

Above, Willie Stern (*right*), Otto Stern's brother, at Rastatt about 1912.
Left, the Altpörtel, Speyer.

Top, Edgar in front of his parents' former store, 1983. *Middle*, Edgar in schoolyard, 1983. *Bottom*, Mariele, Hanna, and Elise, 1983.

Left to right: Ernst (Lore's husband), Millie, Lore, Edgar, 1983.

Above, left to right, Walter and Edgar Stern with the mayor of Speyer, Dr. Christian Rosskopf, 1985.
Left, Edgar with Aunt Helene, 1983.

Top, parade in Schwegenheim, 1985. *Middle*, Emma and Edgar, 1985. *Bottom, left to right:* Walt, Gisela, Otto, 1985.

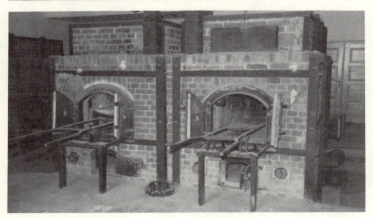

Dachau, 1983.

* * * * *

15

The Holocaust on Our Bread

It was almost two years since my first trip to Germany, and now I was once again enjoying brushing up on my German, talking with German-speaking friends and relatives, and reading a book of children's stories my father had been given on his bar mitzvah.

Milly had told me long before that she would never go back to Germany, but I was delighted that my twenty-four-year-old son, Walt, an English teacher, was going to accompany me.

Walt's bland, positive feelings about Germany, however, made me agitated. He'd been there in 1982 on a tour with a college group, and he was going with me now because he wanted to see the country in depth. But hadn't he listened when I tried so hard to teach him and his sisters about the Holocaust?

"Remember what your people went through at their hands," I now reminded him.

"But can you blame the present generation?" he said.

No, I couldn't. But I also had to push for his deeper understanding of the past. "Please read these," I urged, handing him two of my best Holocaust books. "At least they'll help you appreciate some of my feelings when we're over there." But I wondered if he could. My feelings were so complex, I found it hard to make sense of them myself.

One night, after an hour of childlike absorption in one of the wonderful German stories from my father's bar mitzvah book, I had a dream. Adolph Hitler was giving one of his gutteral German diatribes. Suddenly, I *was* Hitler. Frightened, I turned back into Edgar, and when I woke up I understood the dream's message: How dare I enjoy Hitler's language!

* * * * *

Walt and I arrived in Seeheim on June 26, 1985, and soon found Darmstadterstrasse, where Hugo and Lillian had lived, a narrow street on a hill, lined with rows of quaint, well-preserved houses, some with stores. As I parked, I heard the chiming of a bell—the inviting clang of a large handbell that summons people. Shortly, the air filled with the chant of a deep-voiced woman. Rushing into the square, I saw a ruddy-faced kerchiefed vendor heralding, "*Frisches Gemüse und Obst . . . Bohnen, Kartoffeln, Kirsche.*" It was a moving scene from yesteryear, the harkening of the townsfolk to the street crier, "Fresh vegetables and fruit . . . beans, potatoes, cherries."

We searched to no avail for Hugo and Lillian's house and decided to have lunch. Trying to choose which of three restaurants to go into, I finally picked one more or less at random. When we sat down, something in back of my mind said, this is number 3 Darmstadterstrasse, the house we'd been looking for. I asked the waitress.

"Yes," she replied.

Coincidence? Or was my unconsciousness guiding me through the second pilgrimage?

Despite the restaurant's contemporary amenities—bar, jukebox, "Cocoa-Cola" glasses—I felt it had an aura of the past: stuffed pheasants mounted on the walls, dark-stained paneling adorned with medieval woodcuts and prints, handcrafted bronze light fixtures with dimly lit smoked glass bowls, dark linen tablecloths, china decorated with bucolic old scenes.

As I looked around, something seemed ever so faintly familiar. Or was I reading into it? There was a wood-framed archway that led to a narrow corridor in the back. I couldn't take my eyes off it. When I got up and walked through the archway, I noted a series of glass-paneled doors of thick wood, with latches on top. These were Hugo's meat-storage refrigerators!

I excitedly told the waitress that my relatives had lived here, and she called the owner. When he heard my story, his eyebrows furrowed in deep thought; then his face lit up, and he left saying he'd return shortly. When he did, he asked us to follow him out back: "There is someone there who can give you more information."

As we entered the cobbled yard, an aged white-haired woman shouted from the second story of the house, "Yes, yes, I knew Lillian and Hugo Mayer well. We bought the house from them and made it into a restaurant."

Astounded, I remembered Norman's words about people coming from all over the place to fill my childhood. I asked Walt, "Would 'serendipity' be the appropriate word to describe the incredible coincidences on these trips?"

"It's like there's a hand guiding you," he replied.

When we left the restaurant, I stood for a while staring across the street, wondering from where the Nazis took pictures of people patronizing Hugo's butcher shop. I imagined Lillian and Hugo walking out of their house to leave for America, past Nazis shouting their brutal rhyme about Jewish blood spurting from knives.

* * * * *

We found a guest house on a quiet residential street, where we were assigned a pleasant room with a picture window overlooking lush gardens full of bright flowers. We had arrived in a downpour, but the sun shone brightly when I woke up from a nap. Walt was still sleeping soundly, and I decided to make telephone calls and shop for postcards and souvenirs. The gracious hostess directed me into town.

I walked up the quiet street, breathing in the clean air. What a delightful little town, so peaceful, I thought. Such a contrast to the pictures that formed in my mind outside the restaurant.

The public phones were in the post office. Uncle David was expecting my call to make final arrangements for our visit. He lived in Hagenau, France, not far from Speyer. I hadn't seen him since my family left Germany, but we had kept up some correspondence. I didn't know if he was really an uncle or a cousin, nor through which side of the family we were related. But I knew he was a cantor.

"Lucy and I look forward to having you for the weekend," he told me. "But on Friday it would be better to arrive in the afternoon. We are orthodox; and I have to be at synagogue for Friday evening services."

I also called the mayor of Dolgesheim with whom I had corresponded about an interview, and we agreed to meet the next afternoon.

As I walked through the bustling little shopping district looking for picture cards, I felt as if I could have been in America—except for the buzz of German voices all around, which once more evoked the disturbing images of Hugo and Lillian's last days here.

But I was like a yo-yo: My pleasant mood was quickly restored by the chatter of friendly voices, scenic postcards, colorful Seeheim wineglasses and other souvenirs. And the next morning, I again delighted in a wonderful German breakfast. When Walt's boiled egg arrived cradled in an eggcup, he was amazed. He'd never seen an eggcup before. I showed him how to slice off the top of the egg and spoon it from the shell.

As Walt drove to Dolgesheim, I leafed through my photo album—I was so glad I'd brought it on this trip—and marveled at the snapshot of blonde-haired baby Egon on Uncle Moses' knee, outside the yellow-brick Dolgesheim house. Uncle Moses had a bushy handlebar mustache, a cap on his head, and a cigar hanging from his hand. I recalled his tenderness, punctuated by his constant calm cigar.

Aunt Bertha was a bit taller than he, her body erect, shoulders back. Her face looked somewhat like my Oma's, but it was more effervescent. She had eager shining eyes and a gravelly voice that sort of grabbed you, and that, plus the prominent lump on top of her partly bald head, made me at first hold back a bit when she beckoned me into her arms. I recalled arriving one day as she stood in her immense stone-floored kitchen, which was sort of an annex to the main house. "*Ach, der Egon!*" she shouted, standing at the wood stove stirring a pot of chocolate pudding. Even now my nostrils filled with the aroma, and I hoped today to once again see that house.

I told Walt to follow the road to Hillesheim, where Uncle Moses used to pick us up with his horse and buggy at the train station. There I noted vaguely familiar landmarks—the old brick railroad station with its large sign "Hillesheim-Dondurkheim"; the small yard next to the station house where, most likely, Uncle Moses used to wait for us in his horse and buggy; and the little main street of the village which led to the main road toward Dolgesheim.

As Walt drove out of the village, I watched the pretty fields that flanked the two-lane road. When I saw a steep hill ahead, my heart quickened. "Slow down, this must be the hill," I said, my feet urgently pressing the floor as I re-experienced the thrilling climb that used to bring us to Uncle Moses' house, the first house on the left.

I asked Walt to stop, and surveyed the hill. I walked down, then slowly back up. I heard Uncle Moses' whip crack on the horse. The horse strained up the hill, and from my seat high up in the carriage I felt the scared boyish excitement of seeing the bottom of the road disappear. What would happen if the carriage broke loose?

I drove slowly to the crest of the hill expecting to see the yellow-brick house on the left. The house was not there. All that seemed to remain was a dirt path, probably the old driveway, and a stand of trees. Other houses, apparently built since the war, lined both sides of the street into the village.

I walked over to the driveway. The path was muddy, but I ventured in, hoping for signs of the house. I must have gone a hundred feet when I saw an old iron fence around a small weedy plot. Drawing closer, I saw old gravestones. On the stones were faded Hebrew engravings, and on some of them was the name "Maas." It was Moses and Bertha's family name.

I sprinted over the mud puddles back to the car. "You were right, Walt. A hand is guiding me!" I exclaimed. "I found the family graveyard. Even if I'm mistaken and the house wasn't here, it's incredible that something drew me back there."

"Maybe you were there as a kid," Walt observed.

"I'm going back to take pictures," I said.

"It's starting to rain again," Walt pointed out. "The mayor can probably give you the information later."

"It's not just facts I want. I have to experience these things," I declared. "I'll take the umbrella. And thanks to my German habits, I brought galoshes."

I waded into the hip-high vegetation in the old graveyard. The first headstone read "Alfred Maas." "Alfred Maas! The one she was in love with but couldn't marry because he was a first cousin," I shouted to Walt, who looked on from outside the fence. I hopped from one to the other of the fifteen or so gravestones, pulling off vines, recording the names, photographing.

That afternoon when we arrived at the mayor's house, I stumbled over words apologizing for our lateness. I was looking for the old Maas house, I explained.

"Oh, yes, that still stands," he said, to my great joy. "Before the new homes were built it was the first house on the left. But it was a bit past the crest of the hill. The present owners will show it to you later. But first we will go to the *Rathaus* to search old records about your relatives, then I will take you to a Mr. Eifler, who knew them well."

In the ancient, beautifully restored town hall, he took out huge old ledger books containing detailed, handwritten records of happenings in the village. Despite his busy schedule he waited patiently while I recorded information about the old house, about my relatives' emigration in 1937, about the conversion of the synagogue into a farm storage building, and finally, to my amazement, about a Maas estate in Florida which still sends an annual contribution for the maintenance of the family graveyard.

"Now I will drive by your relatives' house," the mayor said. As soon as I saw it, I clapped my hands exclaiming, *"Da ist es*, that's it—the yellow brick house!"

The mayor dropped us off at Mr. Eifler's house, assuring that we could contact him if we had more questions. Mr. Eifler, a short man in his mid-seventies, was born in Dolgesheim. His healthy, ruddy cheeks brimmed with joy, and his voice, crackling with age, happily gurgled fond reminiscences about the Maas family. For an hour and a half we shared stories and old photos and his Dolgesheimer wine, served in colorful little

The Peppermint Train 145

"Dolgesheim" souvenir glasses that Walt and I had been looking all over for.

I told him my story about the horse and buggy. "Besides being thrilled, I used to be afraid that the buggy would separate from the horse," I confessed.

"That was known to happen," he said, to my complete surprise. I had considered it purely a figment of a child's imagination.

He recalled the names of each of Moses and Bertha's children and nostalgically told of one of them coming back to visit after the war and having dinner at his house.

I told him I'd seen Alfred's grave at the graveyard.

"The one with the lame leg, who always walked with a cane," he said. "He died from the First World War."

"But the gravestone said he died in 1928," I observed.

"Yes, but it was from something he got in the war," he said. "I knew him well. I helped lay his gravestone."

Eifler's cheeks glowed when he saw Hugo and Lillian's photo. "They got married in my neighborhood here. And I met my wife through Lillian, in Seeheim!"

"Astounding," I exclaimed.

"Yes, we were friends with all the Jews. We drove cattle for them. In the winter when one didn't earn much, we earned a little extra doing that. One day I was in Hugo's butcher shop. Lillian introduced me to a friend of hers. We started talking and I invited her to Dolgesheim for the grape harvest. We married a year later, in 1934. Your relatives all came to our wedding. And oh, how already at that time the Hitlerites raised a fuss about Jews at our wedding. But I didn't care."

"Lillian died last year," I told him, "but I spoke with Hugo on the phone a few days ago."

"You must tell him that you met me," he said. "Tell him Scharff, my wife's maiden name. He will remember."

"How many other Jewish families were there in Dolgesheim?" I asked.

He named five that he knew. "And let me tell you what happened to one of them," he said. "I can talk about it now. Frank was found hanged one night. And it was claimed that he had hanged himself. But let me tell you what really happened. I don't have to guard my tongue any more. The Nazis dragged him through town, beat him, and then hanged him. I wasn't around at the time, but I know that where he was hanged, and the way he hung with a pullover on his head, it was impossible to hang oneself. And listen to this: after the war there was a trial for the murder. Frank's skull stood on the lawyer's table with seventeen holes in it where they'd beaten him. But nobody wanted to admit to it. They blamed it on someone who was killed in the war and couldn't come back as a witness."

Eifler sighed. "Bad times they were. I was arrested once, too, for my liberal views. But they released me."

"Yes, good times and bad times we had," he said as we started to take our leave. "But I am so glad that you came to visit me."

As he handed us two bottles of Dolgesheimer wine, Walt asked where we could buy the souvenir wineglasses.

"Right here. For free." Mr. Eifler said, generously handing us two and repeating, "And don't forget. Tell Hugo about me. He will remember."

The driveway of Moses and Bertha's house looked as if it hadn't been touched since I'd been here as a boy. Except for a few old paving stones, it was now all dirt. Further back lay mounds of old bricks and lumber next to an old stone-barn. In one spot stood a lonely looking brick arch, apparently the remains of a doorway to a building. The annex wasn't where I'd thought it was, and there was no trace of the old kitchen. But the current tenants, who were restoring the house, showed me the original stone floors in the old barn, the iron loops where the cattle were tied, and an immense cellar covered with ancient wood planks.

* * * * *

Early Friday morning I visited the public swimming pool to which my mother and Aunt Lillian had taken me though Jews were forbidden. The village where the pool was located looked like a picture postcard: white church spire, red rooftops amid gentle, rich green hillsides. The loveliness of the scene heightened my gloom. As Walt turned into the parking area for the pool, I shrank down into my seat and started to cry. Facing us was a sign, *Zum Schwimmbad* (To the Pool).

Suddenly, the words on the sign changed. They read *Juden*

Verboten (Jews Not Allowed). I was scared. But Aunt Lillian told me that they wouldn't bother children and that she and Mother would be in the woods nearby.

I walked toward the sign. My legs seem to move like a fuzzy slow-motion movie flashback, the legs of an eight-year-old boy. I am thinking, "Will they let me in?" thinking, thinking, "Will they throw me out?"

Suddenly I snapped back to reality, felt the strap of my camera bag on my shoulder, felt the press of my hand around my notebook, saw Walt at my side. I approached the entrance gate and stood silently staring in. The pool was lovely, empty except for two swimmers doing gentle laps in the glistening water.

My eyes searched for the wooden lifeguard hut that was there fifty years ago and for the high diving board from which I saw a girl dive off and hit her head on the concrete edge of the pool. I could still hear the thud. The lifeguard had come running, picked her up, and carried her to the wooden hut. I had worried about the girl and wanted to ask the lifeguard about her, but I hesitated. I was a Jew. A little later, my heart overcame my fear.

Now, a young man came running out of the modern lifeguard building shouting something in German. I felt a stab of fear till I realized he was only saying that we weren't allowed there in street clothing. I told him my story, and he looked amazed.

"Fifty years ago is close to three times my life time," he said.

After showing us around, he rummaged through files for photos of the pool before it was renovated and asked how I liked the pool as a boy.

"I loved it, but things weren't so good for me then," I replied. When he asked what I meant, I said, "There was a sign outside, 'Jews not Allowed.'"

He grimaced, and shook his head. "I could never understand how such a terrible thing could happen in this country, how human beings could be like that."

"I had that same thought coming into this peaceful town this morning." I said.

"I often feel ashamed of my country for what happened," he said. "We young people are constantly reminded of it, on TV, in school. Our bread is buttered with this matter!"

When we said good-bye, he said he wished he could return our entrance fee. "No, no," I waved. "It will help this nice pool."

* * * * *

David and Lucy lived in an apartment next to the orthodox synagogue in downtown Hagenau. We embraced, kissing on both cheeks in French custom. I was thrilled, and Walt seemed awestruck at meeting such ancient relatives. They were dressed up—either for our visit or for the Sabbath—and David wore a yarmulke. Lucy apologized for her apron; she was cooking the Sabbath meals.

Before we could even ask about bringing our luggage up, we sat down and began to reminisce. Since they were orthodox I would not be able to write or use the tape recorder after sundown.

"I remember vividly when I visited you as a child," I said. "Your son had an electric train, and I marveled at that."

Neither of them seemed to recall their son having a train.

"But I'm sure you had a piano," I said.

"Yes, that's true."

"Well, I was about five. And slowly I edged my way over to the piano, and finally got up the courage to raise the lid. My father told me to put it down, but you came over and said it was all right. Then I banged on it. Till you all had enough."

We laughed.

I learned that David, now eighty, was not my uncle but my mother's first cousin. He had been a cantor all his life. "I sang at your parents' wedding," he said proudly.

I was flabbergasted. "Do you still sing?" I asked.

"No more," he said, ruefully. He still took care of the synagogue and helped with the Sabbath services. "Not many people come anymore," he said. "Sometimes they don't even have ten people for a *minyan*." Before the war they had 240 families. Hagenau had been heavily bombed, and when the Jews returned from their internment in 1945 the synagogue was a mess. Months later, it reopened with 140 families. "Now there are only forty," he said, sadly.

"Walt and I will help make up the *minyan* this weekend," I

smiled. David's eyes lit up. "Oh, you will come to services with me?"

"Of course," we said, to David's delight.

He seemed so proud that he still worked for the synagogue. He had been administrator until his second heart attack two years ago, he explained; now he still performs some funeral services and conducts the choir on holidays and festivals. "But one thing I insist on doing," he said with quiet emphasis. "I always assist the rabbi. That I do." David sighed, "At eighty, one is allowed to do so little. But I am glad I came this far. Back in 1945, in internment, when I was so sick with lung poisoning, I never thought I'd make it."

Lucy walked into the kitchen, saying "You tell them about the war. I don't like talking about that."

When the Germans came in 1940 the family fled to Périgueux, a small community in unoccupied France where thousands of Jews gathered, sleeping in barracks and in the forests. When the Nazis took over that part of the country too, things got rougher.

"What happened to you?" I asked.

"Although many Jews hid in the woods, and in private homes," David explained, "many were killed. One time the French resistance shot three Nazis. Forty hostages were taken in retaliation and were shot. Lucy's father was among them. They never did anything to me but I had some harrowing moments," he continued.

He was arrested three times. The first time, the Gestapo took him to headquarters merely as a scare. The second time, they interrogated him for five hours. "But the third time, there was a French policeman with the Gestapo. He was worse than the Germans. When I complained that Lucy's father had been shot, the Frenchman told me that if I'm dissatisfied, they'd shoot me too. Then he ordered me to give him the address of all the Jews living in Périgueux." David was now breathing harder, and his quiet voice took on a stern expression. "'That I cannot do,' I told him. 'That is asking too much of me.' Then the Germans let me go."

Lucy came in from the kitchen, tearful. "My father was sixty-four. Before they shot him he told them that he'd been a German soldier for four years in the First World War. Of course they didn't listen to him."

It took a while for David to resume the subject. When he did, he told of passing a Jewish school one day when the Nazis came and shoved all the children onto trucks. "They never came back, not one!"

"How much did you know about what happened to the Jews who were taken away?" I asked.

"No one knew," David said emphatically. "We knew that they were deported, but no one knew where. Only afterwards, toward the end of the war did we know about places like Auschwitz."

"How did you find out?"

"From people who had jumped off the trains and smuggled themselves back," he explained. "But people were shot in Périgueux," he continued. "And the shootings went on till the very last minute when the Americans were near."

"How did you get lung poisoning?" I asked.

"Exhuming bodies," he said, his voice lowered, and pausing. "It was one of my duties right after the liberation—to expose bodies of those who had been shot. Afterwards, I spent eight months in a sanatorium. Only the One Above saved me."

Before we left on Sunday afternoon, I asked David how he felt now about the Germans.

"We can forgive, but never forget," he replied.

Forgive? I thought. Can we? Should we? The question had special poignancy for me when, en route to Speyer, I decided to visit the memorial grave of my father's relatives at the Jewish cemetery in Mannheim.

We were surprised at the size of the cemetery, a reflection of Mannheim's once thriving Jewish community. The cemetery was surrounded by a stone wall with a locked gate. A sign indicated it was closed on Sundays, but I was determined to see the family memorial so we climbed the fence.

In the solitude of the wooded grounds, I heard only the sound of rustling leaves in a light breeze. We stole silently along landscaped stone paths, by rows of hundreds of ancient and more recent tombstones, until we found the family memorial. I stood grimly staring at the names on the black marble stone, recalling how they died: my father's mother, of natural causes in Mannheim in 1937; Richard, fighting for Germany in 1915; Arthur, in Gurs in 1942; Ino, from an American bomb in 1944; Anna and her daughter Lydia, in Auschwitz.

* * * * *
16

"So Attached Was He Here"

As soon as we arrived at Speyer's Goldener Engel Hotel, I scanned the houses across the street. Which was the one in which I left my grandparents forty-nine years before?

To my astonishment, I had left the address at home. If there's a hand that's guiding me, I reflected, it not only brings good luck but it forgets painful information too.

I started our tour of Speyer just as I had in 1983, with the Postplatz. As we entered the square Walt's face lit up, and I was thrilled to be able to share with my son this pivotal scene of my boyhood—the post office, the Altpörtel, the store, the Dom in the distance. "Now I can appreciate what you were so attached to," he said. "Seeing pictures of it and hearing you talk about it is one thing, but seeing it first hand. . . ."

Spontaneously I heard myself utter the same words as in 1983: "Now I will walk home again." This time though, there was less sadness. Maybe this time I could reclaim more of the joy.

As we approached the old school I noticed that it had been renovated since 1983. Its old brown bricks were now white. But the big wooden entrance door hadn't changed. School was open, and, motioning for Walt to follow, I joined the group of children streaming into the building and strode up the steps I'd first seen on the day of the elections fifty-two years ago.

The lively chatter of young children echoed through the familiar cavernous corridors. I even thought there was a familiar smell in the air. I approached some teachers chatting in the hall. They received us warmly. One of them asked me to say something to her class. Another spent his whole free period with us, chatting and showing us around.

As we left the building, a small boy approached us. "You are from America," he said tentatively.

"Yes," I replied. "Were you in the class I spoke to?"

"Yes," he said with a friendly smile. "You were eight years old when you went to the Zeppelinschule?"

"Yes, just about your age."

"Why did you go to America?" he asked.

"The Nazis didn't like Jews," I said, watching his face.

"Oh," he said, with a puzzled or possibly embarrassed look.

I shook his hand, saying, "But I enjoyed talking to a friendly boy like you."

As we came to my old home, Walt said, "So now I see it with my own eyes, where you lived as a little boy. It looks so nice for such an old house." I showed him the yard, where the chicken coop had been, then rang the bell of the tenants in the second-floor apartment. I had written them, hoping they would show us in.

A middle-aged couple opened the door. As I saw the little foyer, an eerie tingle went through my whole body, and as we walked in, I was almost overwhelmed by the nostalgia of being back. There were the bedrooms, the old kitchen, the little bathroom, all in their places. But how startlingly small the rooms now looked! As we sat down in the living room, a mist formed in my eyes, and I saw my father's enormous desk, the matching dining room set, then a sadder image: my father closing the shutters, hushing us all, turning on his shortwave radio just loud enough to hear with his head close to the set, listening for news from abroad about what was truly happening in Germany.

* * * * *

I was nervous when I approached the secretary in the offices of the *Oberbürgermeister*, Mayor Rosskopf, with whom I'd had a warm correspondence over the last two years. Then as the mayor's door opened, I was seized with terror at the sight of a man so prototypically German: erect posture, strong face, blond hair. He did a crisp right face toward us, stretched out his hand, and as he greeted us with an efficient, *"Guten Tag, Herren Stern,"* I even thought he clicked his heels. Then, his hand held fast to mine, his eyes sparkled with friendliness, and his fiftyish face smiled warmly. I realized that my terror had come from a long time ago. He had not clicked his heels, Walt later told me—he just gave a crisp impression.

"I am so glad I could find time to see you today," Dr. Rosskopf said. "I am sorry it has to be short; I have an important meeting this evening. But I was most interested in your correspondence and your visit to Speyer."

When he asked how he could be of help, I replied, "You have already been of much help" and thanked him for the information he and his staff had sent.

Dr. Rosskopf leaned back and asked me to tell him more about my life in Germany. He listened with interest as I talked about my early childhood in Schwegenheim, my parents' store, my 1983 visit, the places I'd seen.

"How does it feel being back in the *Heimat?*" Dr. Rosskopf asked.

Heimat. A word for "homeland," "native land," but a word that has deeper meaning than reflected in these English translations—perhaps "the place where one's heart is."

"Happy and sad," I replied.

"I can understand that," he said, his eyes showing empathy. "You liked Speyer very much," he continued. "I could guess that from your letters and I can see it today in your eyes."

I told of how I cried when I first crossed the bridge in 1983.

His voice gentle and firm, he said, "It saddens me that you had to leave. It took courage to come back after what happened."

I told of the *Pfefferminzzug* that I rode so often between Speyer, Schwegenheim, and Gommersheim.

"Ah yes! *Das Pfefferminzbähnel,*" he said with warm delight. "I rode it myself before they abandoned it in 1956. And you came back this year to gather more information for your book. What will you call it?"

"*Der Pfefferminzzug,*" I replied.

"*Ach, wunderbar!*" he exclaimed, clapping his hands. "That I will eagerly look forward to." His eyes turning serious and looking intently into mine, he repeated, "That I will look forward to. But *Das Pfefferminzbähnel* would be better."

I smiled, recognizing the folksy, affectionate diminutive as it was used in the local dialect. "It had other names too," I said, "*Pfefferminzzügel, Gäubahn* (District Railway)."

"*Gaübähnel,*" he corrected. "*Und, Pfefferminzbähnchen, Gäubähnchen.*"

"Such warm feelings people have about that train even now," I said.

Dr. Rosskopf picked up his calendar and, to my surprise, invited us to join him for lunch tomorrow. "And I would like to invite the reporters from the newspapers," he added. "Is that all right with you?"

"We will be honored," I replied.

Indeed, I recalled my fantasies, even hopes, of being written up in the Speyer papers.

"And please," he said, "if there is any way I can help,you, do not hesitate."

"There is something," I said. "I neglected to bring the exact address where my grandparents lived on Mühlturmstrasse."

"Yes, I wrote you about that," he replied, looking into his folder. "Number 11."

"Exactly across from the Hotel Goldener Engel! Just as I had suspected!" I exclaimed.

As we got up to leave, I handed him a little box. "Something for you from America."

He beamed as he saw the commemorative medal of George Washington. "I know much about this first American president," he said. "And I will find a place of honor for him on my desk."

In the outer office he handed me a package. "I was going to give you this tomorrow," he said, "but you may want to leaf through it tonight." It was a handsomely illustrated book, *Speyer: Bild einer Stadt (Speyer: View of a City).*

"I have no words for this," I stumbled.

"You can say it in English too. We know a little," he chuckled.

"I am thrilled," I said. But he and his secretary didn't seem to know the word.

"*Etzückt?*" Walt asked, as we struggled for a correct word.

"*Ja. Wunderbar!*" Dr. Rosskopf replied. He then took the book, wrote something in it and handed it back.

When we returned to our hotel I stared across the street at 11 Mühlturmstrasse. I suddenly noticed the dormer windows on the third floor. "That was it!" I exclaimed. "The garret apartment where I said good-bye to my grandparents forty-nine years ago to go to the other side of the world." I looked at it for a long time and I would look at it again and again during our week at the hotel. But when we left Speyer on Sunday, I realized that I had never even inquired about seeing the inside of the apartment. I could not face the pain.

When we got to our room, I translated Dr. Rosskopf's inscription in the book: "To a former fellow citizen, Mr. Edgar E. Stern, and his son, Walter, for pleasant remembrance of the old city—despite the terrible tragedy."

* * * * *

The Ratskeller, where the mayor had asked us to meet him, was a charming cellar restaurant. It had a historic appearance, with a vaulted brick ceiling and walls, clay lampshades carved with ancient scenes, thick oak tables and booths.

The mayor and a reporter received us in a cozy alcove in a side room. Dr. Rosskopf immediately put us at ease. "Did you sleep well at the Goldener Engel last night?" he asked, adding with a smile that he wants to be sure that visitors in Speyer are well accommodated.

"Very comfortable," I said. "Especially since we moved to a room where the street noise is less. And they serve a nice breakfast."

"Ah yes, the street noise. Always a problem in today's

world," he said. "So, today we are very interested in talking more about you and your experiences," the mayor continued. He had briefed the reporter and they both wanted to hear more of my story.

I told of my German boyhood—Speyer, Schwegenheim, Mannheim, Kaiserslautern. Dr. Rosskopf and the reporter were visibly moved as I described my chocolate bar melting in the field of Gommersheim, and their eyes strained as I frankly told what I recalled of saying good-bye to my grandparents, and to Speyer.

Then, choosing my words more carefully, I explained my struggle with positive and negative feelings about Germany. I told them how I cried when I came back to Speyer in 1983 and what joy I found in seeing the familiar scenes of my childhood.

"So attached was he here," the mayor said, with quiet emphasis. "Make sure to write that in your article," he told the reporter.

"In fact, I brought a poem about Speyer," I said. "May I read it?"

"Yes, yes," they urged.

"It is from the book you sent me last year, Dr. Rosskopf, *Geschichte Der Juden in Speyer (History of the Jews of Speyer)*. The poem was written in 1937 by a Jewish man for the jubilee of the Speyer synagogue."

> You were, oh dear old Speyer,
> Wherever I even in the distance stayed
> And whatever the times brought me,
> You were deep in my heart always near,
> The city of my birth and where I once was young
> Remained always a happy memory.

Obviously moved, Dr. Rosskopf said, with emphasis, "I would like to have a copy of that poem." As I handed it to him, he reached for a package. "And this is a good moment to give you another memento from Speyer." It was *Historisches Museum der Pfalz*. Published in 1983, it included photos of Jewish relics in the Pfalz Museum: a Purim plate, a Torah pointer, and a tapestry picturing hundreds of Jewish German soldiers holding a field Yom Kippur service in 1870.

"And here is another pride of Speyer," he said, giving me a gift box of two bottles of Speyer's "Ruländer" wine. He then told us the photographers would arrive in a while. "I wanted us to be finished eating first."

As we ate, I remarked how unusually fine the meal was. And when the waitress came, Dr. Rosskopf told her it was "*Hervorragend!*" I wasn't familiar with the word, but assumed it was the highest compliment, and with a flourish, repeated "*Hervorragend!*"

"*Hervorragend,*" Walt followed.

"Now I would like to ask you a sensitive question," the reporter said. "Were any of your relatives killed by the Nazis?"

"My father's sister and niece in Auschwitz, his brother, various other relatives. And some were in the camps but survived."

My heart hung in suspense in the ensuing moment of silence.

"That distresses me very much," Dr. Rosskopf said, emotionally, turning to the reporter. "That he and his family were so attached to Germany and had to leave, and that others came to such a wretched end. It makes the whole tragedy much heavier in my heart!

"Now make sure you write about that," he added, shaking a finger.

The photographers arrived, and I made sure all the gifts were in view. Then after they and the reporter left, Dr. Rosskopf stayed to finish looking through my album, page by page. As we chatted, I learned that he had a doctorate in law and had become mayor of Speyer in 1969. When I expressed my amazement, he explained that they are elected for a ten-year term, adding with a grin, "and if we do well, the people renew us for a long time."

Afterward, I told Walt of my astonishment at the amount of time the mayor spent with us. "But German officials often honor returning Jews," I added. "There's PR value in this for him."

"But he was so personally warm to you," Walt reminded me. "I felt that, even though I didn't understand most of what he was saying. True, he had the manner of an official, like a teacher, or politician, but I sensed his sincere interest."

"Well, the letters he wrote to me were very cordial, and always prompt," I added. "And just because he holds public office and wants to be known for honoring returning Jews, and maybe non-Jews too, and even if he likes his name and picture in the paper—that doesn't mean he's insincere. I like my name and picture in the paper too."

"And he stayed to chat even after the reporter had left," Walt added. "Just for PR he didn't need to spend almost two hours with us."

* * * * *

As I drove to Kaiserslautern, I had no idea where 23 Fackelstrasse was—the site of Aunt Selma's and Uncle Eugene's store—but "the hand" guided me again. I parked, and found the Fackelstrasse three blocks away. The street was now a shopping mall, closed to motor vehicles. As I scanned the stores I exclaimed, "There's number 23! And after all these years it's still a hat store!"

It was after hours and only an ice-cream shop was open, next door. As I darted around taking pictures, a man with an apron came out of the ice-cream parlor, looked curiously at me a few seconds, and disappeared. Shortly, I walked in after him and told him my story. He literally bubbled over, talking to me in English and German with an Italian accent. His name was Bertolini, and although he'd come from Italy only after the war, he told me, he knew that the hat shop had been there long before.

He went next door with me, and, as the three of us peered into the store a woman appeared from the back. "It's the owner, Mrs. Kleber," Mr. Bertolini said, knocking on the door.

As we entered, a wave of nostalgia swept over me—the hats on stands, the singular smells, the vanities, the mirrors. Mrs. Kleber explained that she now owned the store but that she had worked for the woman who had bought it from my Aunt Selma.

"Incredible!" I exclaimed. "And it used to have two windows," I said, showing my photo of the old storefront.

"We halved it," she explained.

In the back of the store, I faintly recalled Uncle Eugene working on his furs at a big board on sawhorses, and women sewing nearby. "And is the little back yard still there?" I asked, pointing to a photo of Gerd and me playing in it.

"Yes, yes," she said, catching my animation.

When I saw the backyard, I clapped my hands and, delighted, took pictures.

Mr. Bertolini invited us for ice cream, but I explained that before dark I wanted to see the Rundbau, where my aunt and uncle had lived. He told us how to get there, adding "I stay open till 11. Come back and have some good ice cream, and we can talk some more."

The Rundbau had always intrigued me as a child—it was an unusual, circular apartment complex with a driveway around the inside. As soon as I saw it again, I felt catapulted toward it and rushed into the inner circle. There I stood, wondering where Aunt Selma's apartment used to be and staring at the wading pool in the little circular park bordered by the driveway. How well I recalled that pool!

A photo took my mind back to July 19, 1934—my seventh birthday—in Aunt Selma's apartment. They gave me a new bathing suit, embellished with a singular star, urged me to put it on and go down to the pool. When I refused, Uncle Eugene joked, "It was made especially for you, Egon Stern." *Stern* means star.

I recalled that Egon was too shy to go down to the pool. And maybe he was afraid. He'd grown self-conscious about his Jewishness. Other boys and girls had reminded him of it in school. One had even threatened to beat him up. Also, maybe Egon sensed his family's fears, despite their assurances that he'd be all right in the pool. Finally, Egon went down with Aunt Selma when she took Gerd.

The photo had kept this memory alive. It showed me standing in the water, the four-pointed star prominent on my belly, next to the other boys and girls, two of whom were holding little Gerd. One of those boys I remembered especially well. I played with him whenever I came to Kaiserslautern. He had a huge shock of blond hair, and I could even now hear his bubbly, nasal, kind voice and see his twinkling blue eyes that reached out to you. I wondered what had become of that blond playmate. Did he become a Nazi? And those girls so affectionately holding Gerd?

As we started to leave the complex, an older couple passing us said hello, and, seeing my camera and tape recorder, the man asked in broken English, "You interviewing? You American?" Hearing my story, he invited us in, "for talk, and some wine."

He talked about the war, of being forced into the army and having to go to the front. "I not want Hitler," he said in broken English.

"But when in Rome you have to do what the Romans do," I replied, in German.

He shook his head emphatically. "Not like Rome. Here, when not do what Nazis say, they shoot you." He poured more wine, adding "I not guilty."

Afterward, I said to Walt, "No German I've thus far talked to acknowledges they supported Hitler."

"And probably no one will," Walt replied. "If they did, they wouldn't be able to look you in the face."

"He invited us in," I said.

"That was amazing in itself," Walt added. "You spend thirty seconds with people here and they start asking you questions. Like in the bookshop today when the lady was asking about your history."

"Sure. I'd bought a lot of books," I laughed.

"Yes, but it happens everywhere," Walt said.

"At least in the smaller places like Speyer," I said.

"A place with 50,000 people isn't that small," he observed.

* * * * *

"You have hit the newspapers!" the hotel manager told us at breakfast the next morning. "Nice big stories, with your pictures too."

The story was in both Speyer papers. "Heart-rending Love Preserved," read one headline. "A Visit in Speyer and the Results: 'The Peppermint Train,'" read the other.

"It is always moving," Dr. Rosskopf was quoted, "to see how much former Jewish citizens or their offspring are emotionally attached to their birthplace and visit Germany, though they experienced so much suffering here."

My story was all there: Speyer, Schwegenheim, the store, the Peppermint Train, my chocolate farewell in Gommersheim, my "relatives who gave their lives in the concentration camps," and the paradox: "His heart still throbs for Speyer."

* * * * *

17

Reclaiming Boyhood Trains

ON THIS TRIP, one of the things I most eagerly looked forward to was a train and trolley ride to Mannheim. I yearned to hear the roar of that boyhood train again, the clickety-clack of iron wheels, the screeching of brakes coming into the huge Ludwigshafen station, to see the awe-inspiring waiting-hall with its high ceiling. But the fantasy was shattered when I saw the train.

Of course I hadn't expected it to be altogether like in the olden days—a coal locomotive with choo-choo sounds and spumes of steam. But what now rolled into the Speyer station wasn't even a train—it was one car!

But as we pulled out of Speyer, I closed my eyes, and soon, when the conductor announced: "Schifferstadt," I began to smile. Egon always thrilled at the sound of that stop. Now, fifty years later, I discovered why. "*Schiffer*," according to my dictionary, means sailor. Schifferstadt means "Sailor City"—a name to intrigue a young boy.

Sometimes Egon changed trains in Schifferstadt, but when the train went through the station without stopping, Egon would wonder if the conductor forgot.

Today we had to switch trains. This pleased me, for our next train was a big train. No steam engine of course, but at least I would ride again on a big German train. But it was different now, and so were the passing scenes outside. Then, walking into the sleek new Ludwigshafen station, I missed the high, glass-paneled ceiling and the porters with their little wagons. Almost as if to try to bring all that back, I went to the information booth to inquire about the old station. It no longer exists, they told me. Of course, I thought. Ludwigshafen was bombed to smithereens.

However, one sight in this sleek new building did make me feel like a boy: a coin-operated model train. What childish delight I felt, making one train go and another one stop, watching trains cross bridges, slip in and out of tunnels cut through mountains, and hearing choo-choo sounds and even seeing little puffs of "steam."

Outside, we boarded a trolley. They're sleeker now, I reflected. And the electronic bell doesn't compare to the pleasing tinkle of that childhood streetcar. But I imagined the way the trolley once was, and when we crossed the bridge into Mannheim I watched the river flicker between the latticed girders and my spine tingled as I remembered: It was night. Father was holding me, Mother sitting next to us. Multicolored reflections from the river and the city lights blinked hypnotically. And my eyes fought back sleep in the darkened trolley car. Even now, my eyes instinctively closed, till I was startled by the conductor's voice, "*Lindenhof. Umsteigen.* . . ."

Shortly, we got off to visit Aunt Helene. She was so happy to see us that she burst into tears. She felt even more lonely than when I saw her in 1983. "Lore has been dead now over a year," she reminded me, "and now I have no one left."

Walt seemed in awe at this eighty-eight-year-old relative who was still in such good health. I was thrilled to see her again and glad that I wouldn't have to rush the visit as I did in 1983. We spent a long time reminiscing over my old photos.

When Aunt Helene saw the picture of my father's mother standing in front of Uncle Oscar's car, she exclaimed, "That is taken in Mühlheim."

"Mühlheim?" I asked. "Where is that?"

She explained it was outside Mannheim. She and Uncle Willie had a house there. When the Nazis came to power they took the house away from them.

"And did you know, Edgar, that your grandmother died in this home I am now in?"

My mind went back to 1937, at our apartment on Fairview Avenue. A telegram came from Mannheim. It was the first time I saw my father cry. He sent me to get Uncle Oscar, who had come to America just a few weeks before. Uncle Oscar let out a shriek when he saw my father, and they cried together. I recalled that after a while, I started to sing. My father admonished me—"Don't you know that your grandmother just died!"

Seeing the photos of Uncle Willie, Aunt Helene became wistful. "There he is, my Willie, in his First World War uniform. So stately, so fine. And there are the pictures of when your parents visited us in the 1960s. My Willie was still living then, may he rest in peace."

We started to talk about his experiences during the war, and I asked her to tell me how Uncle Willie managed to stay in Mannheim till the last months of the war.

"You know, Edgar, I wasn't Jewish," she said. "And people today ask me if the Nazis didn't bother Willie. Well, our neighbors were unique. They tried to help us." Turning sad, she continued, "But he endured so much in the concentration camp at the end of the war."

She burst into tears, then heaved a deep sigh. "And Edgar, I must tell you this. It is so hard. But I must say it. Lore was at one time so against her father!"

I was stunned. Did I understand correctly? But I couldn't think fast enough in German to ask her to clarify. Lore had told me that she'd protected her father, but she also hadn't wanted to elaborate. I would never find out the truth.

"And here is a photo of my brother-in-law Ino, and his wife," Aunt Helene continued. "Did you know, Edgar, that he was killed in an air raid in 1944?"

"Yes, Aunt Helene, I knew that."

"And here is their only sister, Anna," she continued. "And her daughters, Lydia and Gertrude. Anna was very studious, serious, hardworking. But she was sickly, and almost totally blind by the time the war started. And Lydia, the younger one, had a lung infection. Ino's wife and I went to the Gestapo to try to save them. The Gestapo told us to get out or they would take us too. Later that day we were hauled back and interrogated for two hours."

I imagined the scene at Auschwitz: A line of prisoners, a German officer pointing his baton—Gertrude, who was healthy, to the right to be kept alive to work; Aunt Anna, Lydia to the left.

As I turned the pages of the album, we recovered from the sadness and chatted about our families, about Mannheim, about ourselves. Walt and I marveled at Aunt Helene's health. She still helps in the kitchen, she said proudly, and still goes for walks in the park. "I want to stay in good health as long as I can, and indeed hope to see you again. And please write, Edgar," she said as we left. "Even though I may not answer. You know I don't like to write."

We took the streetcar to the Mannheim train station, which had been rebuilt in the traditional style. I marveled at the huge arched windows on each end, and as I listened to the announcements coming over the loudspeakers I looked up at the high ceiling and mused over my childhood fantasy of God on the other side.

Egon never took a train from Mannheim to Speyer because in those days there were no such direct connections. But today, Edgar did. And during this ride, I pondered: Why had I set aside a whole day just for the chance to ride a German train? I asked myself. Suddenly, my brother-in-law's words rang in my ears: "Ed, you're really making those pilgrimages to reclaim something you lost as a kid."

Yes, today I reclaimed my boyhood trains. But was it really just the trains I was seeking? I asked myself. No, it was what they represented—a happy childhood, fond connections. I could never fully reclaim German trains. Too many were transports to the death camps.

Except the Peppermint Train. How could I ever think ill of that?

No, as Norman said, I really came to Germany to tell Egon

that he did nothing wrong, that he was not responsible for the bad things that happened. To claim my innocence?

Maybe that's why I was so drawn to talk to people who knew me as a child—like the three women who had worked in our store. Having seen the newspaper articles, they'd called me and begged me to visit them, and I'd assured them I wanted to see them as much as they wanted to see me.

Maybe I wanted to hear the people apologize for the past and tell me it wasn't my fault? Is that why I felt such a strong compulsion to visit Konrad and Klaus again even though they hadn't answered my recent letters about my coming to Speyer?

Why had they suddenly stopped writing? Was I too much of a reminder of the ugly past? Did I offend them in one of my letters? I did tell them of our itinerary and mentioned that I'd be visiting Dachau. Did they think that by mentioning Dachau I was rubbing it in? Maybe I was. Why else would I write them about such plans? And maybe they detected my general ambivalence, even though I wasn't aware of it when I was with them. I even drafted a letter to them asking some direct questions about their experience during the Nazi years—what would I have to lose? I asked myself. But I never sent the letter. If those kinds of things could be broached at all, it would have to be done face to face.

But I did comment in one letter that my work on the book was an attempt to reconcile the good and the terrible of the past. Yes, they must have sensed my ambivalence, and assuming they had their own difficulties in facing these matters they probably felt it best to forget it all. In fact I tried to forget it too, but couldn't. I guess I was trying to satisfy this urge for redemption, reclamation. But I promised myself one thing: I would not call them while in Speyer.

However, it happened that while I was showing Konrad's house to Walt, his son came out of the driveway and asked who we were. "I think my father is taking a nap," he said, "but you can go in." "If he wants to call us," I replied, "we're staying at the Goldener Engel."

Konrad did call, and when we visited, Klaus was there too. We talked in friendly tones about a variety of things, and my photo album stimulated our reminiscences. We chuckled as Konrad's wife told us that "the little Peppermint Train crept along so slowly, you could get off, pick flowers, and climb back on." As we looked at a photo of our street, the old Markusweg, Konrad said that it was a dirt road even long after the war, and "when it rained, you sank into the mud. People wore galoshes from the house to where the paving started and then took them off." I told them I wished I had a photo of the old Messplatz. "I saw it yesterday, but it isn't as nice as when we were children." Konrad nodded, saying, "It's smaller and not as pretty." "Fewer trees, and only a couple of chestnuts left," I said. "More asphalt, and lots of noise from the new highway."

As we came to a photo of Aunt Selma's wedding party in 1932, Klaus, seeing himself in it, marveled. "I was only five," he said. "Our mother did the cooking for the wedding," Konrad said, to my amazement. "I remember it well," he went on. "I was out doing errands for my father and couldn't come to the reception, but I attended the ceremony. It was my first time in a synagogue, and I remember vividly how embarassed I felt not wearing a hat. And how surprising it was that people talked in the synagogue! I had been taught to be very quiet in church. I was twelve and didn't really understand how religions could be so different." Then we laughed over how ragged I looked in the picture of Klaus and me on the potato field.

But although we continued to chat pleasantly, I also became aware of feeling a greater coolness from them compared to 1983. Was the friendliness in the throat but not in the heart?

I showed Konrad a photo I had found since my last visit, of him in an army uniform standing next to his mother. "1944, Konrad's last leave," it said on the back. He didn't seem to want to talk about it.

"Someone must have written after all," I said, surprised that our families were not estranged even at the height of the war eight years after we'd left Germany. But Konrad merely shrugged his shoulders. Did he not want to talk about it because of guilt feelings? Or because of the painful seven years he'd spent in a Russian prison camp? Seven years of his youth went down the drain in Siberia, he had told Milly and me in 1983.

Later, though, Konrad did speak of Kristallnacht. His voice

was subdued, but I sensed his strong feelings. "I was in Cologne at the time, and there I saw that terrible destruction of Jewish businesses. All for the excuse of one Jew shooting a German diplomat!" And we got into a discussion of why people voted for Hitler. He built up the economy, put thousands to work; but then Hitler started to do other things, it had gotten to be too late, and the Nazis couldn't be stopped anymore. "And from what happened after that we got our black mark!" Konrad said, nodding his head in emphasis.

When we talked about present-day politics I asked them how they felt about Bitburg—the furor a few weeks earlier over President Reagan's visit to the cemetery where German S.S. lay buried.

They hesitated but replied when I pressed them for their honest views. The S.S. who were buried there, they said, did not volunteer for service. All of them were young people who at the end of the war were taken into the army and were then conscripted into the S.S. You couldn't hold them responsible for what the S.S. had done. "If Reagan had not gone to Bitburg, the Germans would have taken it very badly," Klaus said.

I nodded, thinking, "Can't you also appreciate how we feel about honoring, even by implication, the atrocities represented by those letters S.S.?" I didn't say it because I was afraid the words wouldn't come out right.

Later, when Walt and I chatted about the visit, I commented that my reception had been cooler this time.

"I felt they were friendly and warm," Walt said.

"Wouldn't a former close neighbor and playmate who comes to visit deserve a dinner invitation, instead of just pretzels and wine?" I replied, with some sadness. "Or at least a cake?"

"But it was good wine," Walt replied, innocently.

"We didn't know what they were really thinking," I said.

"They didn't know what you were thinking either," he replied. "And their thoughts did not *have* to be the negative things you infer."

I took this as a sign that Walt couldn't appreciate my feelings, and kept the rest of my thoughts to myself.

Am I making too much of all this? I then asked myself. Many people don't like to write. Friends come and go. And even if they're uncomfortable for all the reasons I've thought about, it doesn't mean they're against *me* or dislike *me*. Maybe it's my paranoia acting up again. Konrad did invite us to his house, and Klaus came over, and we talked. What more should I expect!

The very fact that I'm so bothered by all this proves that I am looking to satisfy an inner need, I reflected, and to reconcile conflicting feelings. But maybe some things can't be fully reconciled, can never be settled. Too much water under the bridge; too much blood in the woods.

I'm learning a lot on this trip but also raising more questions than I can answer even if I spend the rest of my life on them. And maybe there are no answers. But I can try.

* * * * *
18

Noble Man

ON THE WAY TO Schwegenheim Thursday morning, my mind drifted back to 1983: to the trumpeting peasant voice of Elise on the sidewalk across from my grandparents' former house, "*Du bist der Egon!*"; the incredulity on Mariele's face when she pulled up on her bicycle; the exuberant chatter of the villagers who crowded around us; Otto's conscientious interest, his sincere letters afterward, and his continued urgings for me to come back for Schwegenheim's anniversary celebration.

"Otto already feels like a friend," I said to Walt.

I drove into the village slowly, as I had two years before, tingling with childhood memories as I showed Walt the *Eckhaus* and my grandparents' house. Otto was outside waiting for us. He and Gisela greeted us, got to know Walt, asked about Milly and Aunt Selma. Then Otto launched into our schedule for the next few days: a tour of the village this morning and a reception by the mayor to receive the millennium commemorative book; this afternoon a radio interview; tomorrow morning a trip to Gommersheim, a *Festbankett* (festival banquet) in the evening; Sunday, a big parade. "For that you will have to get here very early since all roads to the village will be shut," Otto stressed. "Even the *Pfefferminzbähnel* will be in the parade."

"Oh, I'll look forward to that," I said happily.

"We knew you would," Gisela said.

"Now let me tell you," Otto continued. "Mariele, with whom you were to stay, is so sorry she is in the hospital. She said you can stay with her sister-in-law." He apologized for not having room in his house, since their son was staying with them.

I explained that we preferred to stay in Speyer, and Otto nodded understandingly. As I was to learn over the next few days, Otto had many sides to him. He could be intense, even fervent, but also relaxed, accepting, quite philosophical, and light and jovial.

"But we would like you to eat with us," Gisela said.

"And we know you want to talk," continued Otto. "We will tell you as much as we know."

I thanked them for all they had already written me, then asked about Elise and the others I had met in 1983.

Elise is ill and housebound, they told me. Everybody wants to talk with me again, and the families who now live in my parents' and grandparents' houses want to show us around.

Gisela asked if Walt understood German.

"*Ein bisschen*," he replied.

"He's learned more than a bit of German these last few days," I chuckled.

The conversation soon turned to my family, and to the Nazi era. "My parents were friends of your grandparents," Gisela said, affectionately. "Even as children we used to call your grandparents Loui and Lina." She remembered my grandfather's two cousins, who were friends of her family and used to come to dinner, and also my Uncle Leon.

Gisela had been inconspicuous in the crowd in 1983, and I'd hardly remembered her. Now, I got to know her as a shy, pleasant, kindhearted woman. She appeared seventyish, a bit older than Otto.

"By the time you and your family left, things had gone very far," Gisela pointed out. "And we could do nothing any more. My father was arrested for his political beliefs. Others were arrested for merely talking with Jews." In hushed tones, she recalled a Jewish couple who were "taken away" from Schwegenheim. "A bus came. There were people already in it—other Jews. I remember seeing Rebecca and her husband ordered onto the bus. They had blankets under their arms."

"Did you know of the killings in the concentration camps?" I asked.

"No one knew," they both said, almost in unison.

"Everyone thought the Jews were taken away to work somewhere," Gisela said, "to be protected."

"The people did not want what was going on," she continued, quietly. "But we couldn't do anything about it any more."

"When Hitler started, the country was in a depression," Otto said. "Lots of unemployment, and hunger."

"And he told the people, *'Es gibt Arbeit und Brot'*," added Gisela, "and when people heard him promise work and bread, everyone said, 'We need him. We will vote for him.'"

"Thousands and thousands of men were put to work," Otto said. "They built the first Autobahn by hand. No machines were used."

"So Hitler got good votes from that," Gisela said. "But when he was in power, the other things started. And what he did to the Jews, and to the churches, the people did not want."

"And once he was in power, if you didn't do what he said, you were punished, or killed," Otto added.

"Everywhere were signs 'Don't buy from Jews,'" Gisela continued in quiet tones. "In Speyer, the stormtroopers stood here, there and everywhere and people did not have the courage to go into Jewish stores. The ordinary people did not agree with it, but it was risky to go against the orders. They didn't do anything to you on the spot, but they might be taking pictures of you." Her voice became more emphatic. "Above all, one feared being sent to Dachau. Like the time when my father was arrested. It instilled fear in all of us."

"Everyone knew of Dachau?" I asked.

"Yes. They told us how they terrorized people there—to keep us in line. But we did not know of the camps where the Jews were killed," Otto said decisively. "That was a big secret till toward the end of the war. I was drafted into the army too and

The Peppermint Train   173

was on the Russian front. And we soldiers knew nothing of the camps. Nothing."

Otto said something about the persecutions having begun in 1936. Here I felt I had to set the record straight. "But Hitler had announced it already in *Mein Kampf* in 1925," I said. "And the Nuremberg laws came out in 1935."

"But in 1936 he installed it out and out," he said.

Is Otto saying no one knew of what was going on till 1936?

"And that's when it got to be too late," Gisela said. "Everyone in the village said it wasn't right, but one could do nothing."

"It was all wrong," Otto said intensely. "Nobody realized it, but it was all wrong. Now let me tell you something. My father had a proverb: 'Attack not the church, attack not the Jew, attack not the industrialists.' Do you know what that means?"

As I hesitated, he explained, "If you attack any of these, society goes kaput, totally kaput."

"Like what happened here," Gisela added.

"My father was a social democrat," Otto continued, his voice rising, "and during the dictatorship of the Third Reich he was imprisoned three times. The Nazis knew he was against the war, and when Germany conquered Belgium in 1940, one of them proudly challenged my father with 'What do you think about our war *now*, Mr. Galle?' My father told him, 'We are having victories, but we will not win the war.' Three hours later they arrested him.

"My father taught me well. All my life my mind was clear about people," Otto continued, his face a fervent red. "I am on equal terms with any person, any people, any race. We all come naked into the world. And I want to tell you another proverb my father taught me. It comes from the 1914 creed of the International Red Cross. My father repeated it often, and it is my philosophy: '*Edel sei der Mensch, hilfreich, und gut.*'"

I didn't understand the words at first, and Otto repeated them, drawing out the vowels for emphasis, resonating the German consonants in his throat and on his tongue: "*E . . . del . . . sei . . . derr Menschhh, Hilf . . . rrreich, und Gu . . u . . t*" (Noble, man should be, helpful and kind).

A little while later, Gisela cocked her head toward me and

Walt and said, hesitantly, "Now I want to ask you about something different. Will you eat lunch with us today?"

Somewhat surprised, since I thought that was already understood, I replied slowly, "It is up to you," adding quickly, "We'd be glad to."

"We want you to, but I have to ask you," she started.

Now I knew what she was going to ask, but I waited.

"I have to ask you what you eat, and what you don't eat."

"We eat everything," I interrupted.

"Pork, too?" she asked.

I nodded and looked at Walt. He had understood and said, "*ja.*"

Gisela sighed with relief. "I had to ask. I knew that many Jews eat no pork or even meat that is not kosher. Like your grandparents." She recalled that my Uncle Leon used to eat both. "As long as your grandmother didn't know," she chuckled. "Well, I tell it just the way it was," she added shyly.

"Oh yes. That is best, that we can talk honestly," I said.

"I asked Otto and we decided we would wait till you are here to ask you. I wouldn't want to have cooked something that you wouldn't eat," she said.

"We keep our faith, but we eat anything."

"Alla," Gisela sighed.

"Alla?" I asked, puzzled at the expression. "That is Arabic."

Otto laughed. "Yes, Alla. It's a German expression too, at least around here."

"Alla!" I said. "Only I don't eat much fried food, or butter, and I don't eat sweets."

"We don't eat much fried either. But cake? I baked some special German cake. You will eat that?" she beckoned shyly.

"Since you baked it, I will happily cheat on my diet," I laughed.

"Alla," Gisela sang.

"Alla," Walt and I chanted.

At lunch, Otto told lighthearted proverbs and stories. "*Wenn man Wein trinkt und ein Lied singt, dann ist es herrlich auf der Welt*" (When one drinks wine and sings a song, it is a glorious world), he toasted.

When Walt and I praised their delicious cutlets and fresh

home-grown vegetables, Otto declaimed, "When God created the world, He stayed overnight in the Pfalz and said that in the morning He would need something to eat. So, during the night, God made grapes, corn, wheat, potatoes, lemons, figs, almonds; and all other good things did God bestow upon the Pfalz that night. When He awoke, and ate, He said, 'This beautiful Pfalz is the loveliest little spot on the earth.'"

* * * * *

The book the mayor gave us, *1000 Jahre Schwegenheim, 985–1985*, consisted of 430 pages of village history, carefully detailed and illustrated, including sections on agriculture, industry, schools, population, woods, and churches. I was thrilled with the scale drawing of the locomotive of the Peppermint Train, and I was amazed to find a nine-page section about the history of the Jews of Schwegenheim, as well as four old photographs of stores owned by the Walther and Loeb families. One of them showed my grandfather standing with little Mariele in the doorway of his store, my uncle Leon leaning against the window in which my mother's hats were displayed. "This picture must be from about 1925!" I exclaimed. Walt was amazed to find photos of his ancestors in a published book. "Your family must have been an important part of Schwegenheim," he observed.

As Otto showed us Schwegenheim's busy Main Street, where "16,000 cars pass daily and a bypass is being erected," I finally realized that this was no longer Egon's quiet little village. That world of the stone house, the wood stove, the chicken and geese in the yard, was gone forever.

And I found myself suppressing discomfort when Otto pointed out houses that were once owned by Jewish families, referring to them as *"Ein Jüdishes Haus"* or *"Ein Judenhaus."* The words were familiar to me, but why is a house where Jews lived still being called "a Jewish house?" I recalled how I felt about streets called Judengasse. Ed, you're making too much of it, I told myself. Otto wouldn't use a pejorative expression about Jews.

Otto showed us where the synagogue had been. Seeing my pained, pensive expression, he stood quietly with Walt. My reverie took me back to when I was about four years of age. My grandfather is conducting a synagogue service. I hear him chant in his trilling tenor voice, now soft, then rising, then submerged as the congregation joins in—the men with huge prayer shawls over their heads, their bodies swaying back and forth—then Opa's beautiful solo again, and finally he and the congregation spiritedly join together in the crescendo of the hymn's conclusion.

When we arrived for the radio program, which was broadcast from outdoors, adjacent to Schwegenheim's new 4,500-seat civic hall, the town band and choir were rehearsing, and people were gathering around picnic tables set with colorful placemats. The placemats were blazoned with a cartoon rompingly entitled "*Auf der Walz' durch die Pfalz!*" It was the title of the radio program, "On the Road Through the Pfalz." In this festive air, I felt a fraternal glow.

A woman approached us, saying in typical Pfalz dialect, "*Doh is de Egon.*" She introduced herself as Emma, Elise's sister, explaining she had met me in 1983, wanted so much to talk to me, and was so glad I could come back again. She spoke with an urgent quality, drawing out her words, which were sad at times as she reminisced. "*Ja, ja, Egon,*" she drawled. "I was ten years old when you were born. I helped teach you to walk. I knew your family so well. We lived across the street. We were always together. And we girls spent so much time with your Oma and Opa."

The radio announcer came over to tell me that I would be interviewed as "a former Schwegenheimer." At the sound of the station identification, the crowd hushed, the band played, the choir sang "*Frieden*" ("Peace"), followed by an American gospel song, "We are going to see the king, Hallelujah. . . ." A cute little blond girl recited a poem about farm life, followed by a succession of interviews with people from all phases of life in the village. The author of *1000 Jahre Schwegenheim* discussed the hard work and research that went into the book. Then, as the band burst forth with a rousing march about forests and woods, I was so carried away that I sang along with the camaradic refrain, and then sat enthralled as they sang *Das Pfälzerlied*—the anthem of the Pfalz.

When the former Schwegenheimers were called up, a woman from Virginia spoke of her amazement at how the *Dorf* had been modernized since she left thirty years ago. I mused over the word *Dorf*—it means "village" but has such a cozy, intimate ring to it.

When the announcer introduced me, I was so nervous that I hardly gave him a chance to ask me a question. "I wrote something down since my German isn't so good," I began. "The most meaningful experiences of my visits to Schwegenheim after fifty years in America are the meetings with former friends who knew my family and who helped raise me, as well as the present Schwegenheimers. All the people my son and I have talked to are so warm to me, as it always was, through bright and darker times." I told how I remembered the woods, the *Hutzele*, and the most endearing thing of all, the *Pfefferminzbähnel*, at which the audience applauded, the announcer said if he weren't holding the microphone he would also clap his hands, and everyone cheered.

As I went back to my table, a well-dressed man stopped me. "It was wonderful what you said," he told me, with a sincere look. He continued in an urgent tone, "And please, when you get back to America tell your people that we are their friends. I mean it, sincerely. Tell them we are their friends. It is very important."

Others also told me my remarks were nice, but I sensed Otto holding back. Did he feel uncomfortable about some of the words I had spoken? I knew I did.

When the radio show ended, there was a surge of chatter. Emma and her friends started reminiscing about Aunt Selma, Loui and Lina, Leon, my parents, other Jews of the village. In the hubbub of the dispersing, chattering crowd, I didn't catch much of what was said. Emma seemed to be talking about how the Jews of the village fared in the bad times. I heard her say, with an air of sadness, "Yes, yes, when one thinks about all the suffering," then words got lost again in the babble. But I knew she was still talking about the Jews when I heard someone interrupt, "That's all over!"

Was that remark meant to assuage guilt feelings, I asked myself, or to end the painful conversation? Or both?

But Emma continued. "Yes, yes. But Egon was here two years ago too, and he and his wife were well received by everybody. And now too, with his son."

Then I heard her say, almost as if to herself, "And maybe I too am now forgiven." I would never forget those words.

On the way back to Speyer, I asked Walt about what I'd said on the radio.

"You were a resounding success," he said. "I was impressed, and proud."

"But what about my remark that all Schwegenheimers were warm and friendly even in the darker times. It implies that no one was against the Jews. That's impossible! What made me say it?"

* * * * *

When we arrived back in Schwegenheim Friday morning, Otto declared, "Dear God has brought us good weather for the festival week."

I laughed. "You told us that He favored the Pfalz with everything good!"

When Walt mistakenly addressed Gisela with the familiar pronoun *"du,'* I corrected him but then said, "We are friends and I wouldn't mind if we call each other *'du'"* They were delighted.

On the road to Gommersheim, Otto drove through the village of Weingarten, stopped at a brook, and pointed to the remains of a brick-faced enbankment. "What you see there was part of the trestle that carried the *Pfefferminzbähnel* across the brook."

An image came to mind. The Peppermint Train labored up the embankment, and as it swayed on the trestle, Egon looked down and wondered if it would fall into the water.

Back in the car, Otto said, "The next village is Freisbach."

Suddenly, I imagined the voice of the train's conductor, "Schwegenheim . . . Weingarten . . Freisbach . . . Gommersheim." Those were the stops I must have listened for on that June day in 1936, my last ride on the *Pfefferminzbähnel.*

Expectantly, I looked around for train tracks. I asked Otto.

"They were all taken away, and melted down," he said.

I felt a lump in my throat. But soon I was rewarded with another sight. At the outskirts of Gommersheim, Otto stopped to show us a three-story house. "So," he said, pointing proudly. "Now you can see where you used to get off the *Pfefferminzbähnel* in Gommersheim."

I could not believe my eyes. The house was a modern residence, curtains in the windows "This was the train station?" I exclaimed.

"Yes," he replied, showing us an original baggage shed, and an old water pump that was now a historical site.

"Since we're at the station," I said, "I'd like to walk into town, just like I did that last time in 1936."

The route to the Loeb house did not look at all familiar, and the walk was longer than I expected. But my heart leaped when I saw the street that I never forgot. My eyes darted forward to locate the house, then to the edge of the village. There was the same field where my chocolate bar melted.

I walked on in a trance, till Otto turned into the yard of his cousin who knew the Loebs and who would show us their house. Mr. Bein, who was eighty-three, was sitting with his wife in their cobblestone yard shelling peas into a big tub. A mound of peas lay in a big apron over Mrs. Bein's lap. Hard of hearing, she had trouble understanding who Walt and I were. "From the Loebs. The Loebs," Otto and Mr. Bein shouted into her ear. "Relatives of the Loebs who lived up the street," they tried again.

Finally, she nodded, "*Ach, ja. Von de Judde.*"

I tensed. She had said, "Oh yes, from the Jews." There seemed to be a flicker of embarrassment on Otto's face, too. Or, was I reading something that wasn't there? Wasn't "*Judde*" used for Jews by some Germans like "niggers" for blacks in America? But "*Judde*" is also dialect or colloquial for the plural "*Juden*," I reasoned. But why would someone say "Oh yes, from the Jews?"

Nonetheless, we all sat down and had a friendly chat over my old photos.

Mr. Bein was a mild, kind man. Remarkably chipper for his age, he led us up the street to where my relatives used to live. "I remember when you and your family would come to visit," he said.

When he pointed to the house, I was puzzled. I had expected a yard enclosed by a white cement wall and a big wooden gate, as there were in the photograph.

"Where is the gate?" I asked.

Mr. Bein did not recall a gate. How could I doubt his memory? I was only eight when I was here.

Walt came to the rescue. He showed us the old photo in the album. There it was: the white cement wall and Uncle Julius by the big wooden gate. Now Mr. Bein remembered—they were taken down long ago.

Another photo showed the old concrete step at the entrance door. "The step is still there," I exclaimed, picturing Uncle Julius opening the door when I returned from the field, his big, bald head looking down at me, his face grinning kindly, "we've been waiting for you."

As we walked back, Mr. Bein pointed to another house. "That was also a *Juddehaus*," he said.

That word *Judde* again! It *must* be a colloquialism, I concluded. Yet, I could not shake my discomfort.

I had hoped to relive Egon's walk to the field. But Otto was anxious to go on to other important things to see, and Emma was expecting Walt and me for a midday dinner. Driving past the field, Otto slowed down for me. As I pointed my camera through the back window, I again saw the chocolate oozing to the ground, and I bid a silent good-bye to Gommersheim.

* * * * *

Shortly, Otto parked at the edge of the road and took us into the woods. "This path goes straight to Schwegenheim," he explained, setting a fast pace. "I am taking you to your favorite woods."

Soon, I noted an increasing number of pine trees, and looking toward the ground, I suddenly shouted *"Hutzele!* Walt, these are what we used to collect in the woods when I was a kid!" I stooped to examine one of those *Hutzele* that I hadn't seen in over fifty years and was startled. "This is an ordinary pine-cone!" I'd had such a romantic notion about a *"Hutzel,"* and it turned out to be a plain, ordinary pine cone!

I picked it up, turned it slowly between my fingers, then held it to my nose and breathed deeply in. No, this was not an ordinary pine cone for me. I tucked it gently into my camera bag to take back to America.

We marched on, the echoing crunch of pine needles under our feet bringing to mind a delicious sense of other hikes in these and other German woods.

Otto stopped, pointing to a yellow-green bush with hairy leaves. He grinned. "Do you know what *Brennessel* are?"

"Indeed," I said, my mind flashing back to the age of five, my grandfather on his three-wheeler, me on my *Vierrad* nearing our Speyer house. Suddenly my *Vierrad* slipped off the edge of the road into a thicket of *Brennessel.* Instantly my skin burned from head to foot, and we rushed home. I laughed as I retold the story.

"Try it," Otto urged, rubbing a leaf between his fingers. "It'll burn only a short time."

Almost instantly I felt it. "It burns a lot more than you said, Otto," I laughed. "The last time I felt this was over fifty years ago."

"And from your looks, Egon, your very last time will be today," Otto quipped.

Presently, we came to a wide clearing that ran through the woods. Otto stopped and turned to Walt. "This, Walter," he said, "is where your father used to ride into and out of Schwegenheim on the *Pfefferminzbähnel."*

As my eyes widened, Walt replied, "I think he has been waiting to see this for a long time."

"The clearing looks the same now, Egon as it did when the *Pfefferminzbähnel* ran through it," Otto said, as I stood entranced, "except for the track bed."

Abruptly, I started to walk down the clearing. Walt and Otto followed. Otto was explaining some other things, but I was so absorbed in images of my little train that I hardly heard his words. Suddenly I moved my feet in a fast-forward shuffle, made three short whistle-sounds, then "beep-beep, beep-beep," "sh, sh, sh . . . sh, sh, sh," faster and faster, to the rhythm of the imaginary locomotive.

I turned, shuffled back, and shouted, "Then it clinged—Cling, cling, cling. Isn't that right Otto, it clinged. And whistled. Toot, toot, toot."

"Yes, yes," Otto replied. "As soon as it came to a street crossing it would whistle. And when the train came from Speyer, Egon," he continued, joining my excitement, "it panted and snorted."

"And would black smoke come through the windows so that you had to cough and clean your eyes out?" I asked.

"Cinders," Otto followed. "From the coal. And they hurt!"

As we hiked back to the car, Otto sensed my complete pleasure at this morning's experiences. "I think," he said, with pride in his voice, "no, I will say I really believe, that with this morning's tour I was a big help to you."

"I can't find the right words to express how much this meant to me," I said.

"I am happy that I did something good for you," he continued. *'Edel sei der Mensch, hilfriech, und gut.'* That is a maxim many people on this earth do not know or do not follow. But that is what I did for you this morning, 'Noble, man should be, helpful, and kind.'"

* * * *
19

The Horrible Ambivalence

OF THE MANY PEOPLE who helped fill in my childhood, Emma was one of the most informative. During the two hours Walt and I spent with her and her husband, I got a clear sense of the relationship between my family and their Christian neighbors.

At times she and her sisters didn't have enough to eat, Emma said, almost mournfully, "and your Oma, Lina, came over with her pot saying 'Children, look here, I have some leftovers.' Sometimes we would go over and ask for a piece of bread, and we were never refused. Your Opa would use our barn sometimes to milk his cow and goats, and he would always hand us a package of pudding from his store, saying, 'Here children, make yourselves something sweet.' Yes, yes. We would have suffered much hunger if Lina and Loui hadn't helped us out," she sighed. "And such a thing one doesn't forget. Isn't that right, Egon?"

Is she expressing guilt? I asked myself, or is she trying to revive the good feelings—as I myself have been doing?

Emma continued, drawing out her words nostalgically. "Right inside the back door of the house hung Lina's pots and pans, and we'd sometimes race by and bang on them. And how your Oma would scold us; always good-naturedly. But she was strict about one thing. On the left were the dishes for dairy and on the right were the ones for meat. Each set had its own towels, and when we helped we'd sometimes get them mixed up, and Lina would shake her fists at us and exclaim, 'What are you children doing; now you got me all mixed up again.' But she was always good-natured. And on Passover they had different dishes too. And do I remember how we used to eat their matzos. Oh, what matzos they had!"

When Emma saw the photos of my grandfather, she exclaimed, "Oh look at this picture of your Opa, sitting on his *Hocker* in the yard, with you on his lap. Oh how good Loui always was with the children. He'd sit on that chair of his in front of the store and when a child would go by he'd always say hello. His cane was always under the chair. I remember that we children always thought of him as Santa Claus, with his big beard, his cane, his crippled leg."

"I understand his leg was crippled by a horse," I probed.

"In the First World War," she said, to my surprise, since he would have been already fifty years old at the time. When I questioned her statement, she reflected, "Well maybe not, but as children we always said it was from the war."

"But then he had a second injury," I said. "From a cow, wasn't it? I know only a story that a cow fell on him, but do you know what really happened?"

"Leon brought a cow home," she explained, "and it was tied to one of those iron rings in the yard. Loui used to tease us, saying we'd be tied to those rings if we were bad. Well, Loui looked the cow all over, front, back, and underneath, when suddenly the cow kicked out with all its might."

Finally, at the age of fifty-eight, I knew the true story about the cow falling on my grandfather!

Every page of the album brought more touching stories about my family and their neighbors. "Look at the old *Eckhaus* there, with the grapes growing all over it, and the little washhouse right next to it. That shed is still there. And oh, how I remember when we children used to take baths in that shed and in your house!" My parents, she explained, were the only ones in the neighborhood that had a bathtub—a long, thin tub that was used in the washhouse in summer and brought into the house in winter. "Lina used to fill it, pail by pail with hot water, tell us girls to come over, and put us in the tub three at a time."

Emma then told a fascinating story about my family's millinery business in Schwegenheim. My mother and Aunt Selma would pack their sample hats into big cardboard boxes, tie the boxes onto huge bicycle racks, and ride for miles to customers' homes. When the hats were completed, Emma and other girls would deliver them. "I remember delivering a hat once in Lingenfeld, a beautiful hat," smiled Emma. "And the woman didn't pay for it. I must have been sent back ten times, but they never paid. But everybody asked the woman where she got that beautiful hat, so lots of new customers came from it."

When Emma saw my baby pictures, she exclaimed, "Oh look. There you are inside a circle between me, Mariele, and Selma. We were teaching you how to walk. One of us held you by the hand, the other would say, 'Hop march, hop march.' You'd go two steps at a time. And we'd shout into the house, 'Oma, see how Egon is walking.'"

"And what beautiful curls you had. Light blonde," she continued. "And blue eyes."

"I looked real German," I said.

Emma laughed. "We would tease your mother: 'Elsa, where did you find him. That is not a *Juddebübel* (Jewish boy).'"

I smiled, but thought, "There goes that *Judde* word again. Oh, come off it, Ed! It's dialect. And she said it with such affection."

"*Ja, ja,* Egon," Emma went on. "I was ten years old when your mother brought you home from the hospital."

"On the *Pfefferminzbähnel*," I nodded vigorously.

"*Ja, ja. Mit dem Pfefferminzbähnel,*" she affectionately drawled. "You rode that *Pfefferminzbähnel* so much. After your parents opened their store in Speyer, they would take you with them and bring you back in the evening."

"And after they moved to Speyer I stayed here, didn't I?" I asked.

"They said that once you learned to walk you could stay with them in Speyer. But your Oma often took you to Speyer to see them. And even after you moved, you came back many times to stay with your grandparents. Yes, yes, Egon. Back and forth, and back and forth you went on that train."

I was heartened beyond belief at her words. Someone confirmed, without prompting, the centrality of the train in my boyhood. I wasn't imagining it!

"Yes, yes," she said nostalgically. "I don't think anyone rode that *Pfefferminzbähnel* more than you, Egon."

I had learned a lot today, I reflected. But I needed to know about my Uncle Leon. After broaching the subject, I said, "I heard that he was the black sheep of our family."

Emma hesitated, saying he was always nice.

"Honestly. Wasn't he difficult at times?" I probed.

She admitted that he had a short temper. He yelled at his wife—often about meals because she kept kosher and wouldn't cook the pork he brought home. "Leon was so hot-tempered he'd shatter windows, but five minutes later he'd be the nicest person."

Emma explained that even after my grandparents moved to Speyer and Leon took over the store, she continued to buy from him. "But a stormtrooper man told me I would wind up in a coffin if I continued to buy from Jews. I was only a child. So what could I do, Egon?" she added. Again, I sensed the guilt feelings in her, almost a begging for forgiveness.

Emma's drawl took on a sadder tone, as she told of what happened to other Jewish people in Schwegenheim. She spoke as if she was reliving each scene, in a quietly dramatic way that brought images of those long-forgotten people to my own mind. "Yes, yes, Egon, how I remember: Clara . . . Benjamin . . . Truda . . . Gottlieb. . . . They went to America early enough and didn't have to suffer. But there were those who were less fortunate. Like Hermine. She was bedridden, and I used to go up the street to her house and clean and care for that old woman. But when we were told not to talk to Jews anymore, I just didn't know what to do. One day I looked down at old Hermine lying there in her bed, and she must have seen the look in my eyes, because she said to me, 'Emma, you are still talking to me?' And I said to her, 'Hermine, I'm not allowed to help you any more.' And she answered, 'Emma, I know you can't.' So I went to one of the leaders in the village, who was a teacher of ours, and said, 'What should we do, we can't just let that poor woman lie there like that.' And do you know Egon, what that teacher said to me? He told me to look after the woman as long as she is here. And soon they took her away."

Emma's husband, Phillip, who had up to now been mostly listening to our conversation, told about a couple named Sarah and Max. They were beloved by everyone in the village but were taken away like the rest. They survived and came back after the war to live in Schwegenheim.

"And they died here," Emma said, looking at me as if wondering what I was thinking. "They are buried in the next village, Weingarten."

Phillip told of his consternation when he saw the synagogue and Jewish businesses being destroyed during *Kristallnacht*. He had never been for "all that hullaballoo," and when he complained about what they were doing, the Nazis threatened him. When he got his draft card, it was stamped "Politically Unreliable." But he was drafted anyhow, at seventeen.

After the war, ex-Nazis asked him to sign their denazification papers—to prove they weren't Nazis any more. "I gave no signatures," he said, "even though I knew some of them wouldn't get their jobs back without signatures."

"But Max couldn't turn them down," Emma said.

Stupefied, I said, "You mean the Jewish couple who came back here from the concentration camp signed denazification papers?"

"Yes," Phillip said, "I told Max that he was making a great mistake giving everyone his signature."

"But let me tell you what they told us, Egon," Emma said. She made her voice sound almost as if Sarah and Max were themselves speaking: "'Listen, Phillip and Emma, we want to tell you . . . that everything is over, that everything is past. We don't want to fight bad with bad. We want to continue living here. We are getting old and getting a pension.'"

Walt had been in the next room helping Emma's niece with some English. When he returned, we chatted about our current lives, and then began to take our leave. Emma asked me to give regards to my wife, whom she had met in 1983. "But tell me again," she said. "What is her name?"

"Milly," I said.
"Is she Jewish too?" Emma asked.
"Yes."
"But she is a nice person," Emma said.
My face froze. Jewish . . . *but* a nice person, I heard her say!
Driving back to Speyer, I argued with myself. Maybe there was no "but." Maybe the words were merely, "She is a nice person."
I asked Walt.
"Even if Emma said it," he replied, it's no different than what one hears throughout the world, about Jews, blacks, others."
I nodded. He was right. It is part of the essence of prejudice. Yet, that doesn't make it right. I'd prefer to think I misheard Emma's words, but I will never know.

* * * * *

My experience at the *Bankett* Friday night brought out more ambivalence.

The *Bankett*, designated as the official opening of Schwegenheim's anniversary-festival week, was held in the *Sporthalle*. The hall was bedecked with hundreds of geraniums, and it was filled with people around long tables. The mayor of the village hosted the program, consisting of many speeches alternating with musical, choral, and dance performances. Short-order food and drinks together with the music created a festival atmosphere. Periodically, "shushes" toned down the chatter of the audience.

During a pause between speeches, the mayor came down from the stage and asked me if I cared to make some remarks. I accepted; but this time I confined myself to thanking Schwegenheim for its hospitality and its friendliness and gave "regards from my Aunt Selma."

Back at my table, a man came over, took my hand, looked at me with sincere eyes, and, with a friendly fervor in his voice said, "I must tell you something. I was born in 1930. After the war I lived in Texas a few years and attended Rice University. I must tell you that as a child I saw terrible things happen here in Germany to some of my Jewish friends, and I felt terrible about it. Terrible. And I still do. I had to tell you this."

At the banquet's closing, everyone stood up for the German national anthem. I stiffened when I heard the very same tune to which Germans used to sing *"Deutschland, Deutschland über Alles, über Alles in der Welt"*; a childhood scene again flashed before my eyes: a gathering of school children in a movie theater, their arms outstretched to Hitler on the screen, their voices singing, *"Deutschland, Deutschland über Alles"*; my lips sealed, my arm starting to rise, my face hot with anxiety as Jewish classmates whispered, "You don't have to" and Lehrer Marx's eyes signaled, "Don't."

In the spring of 1985, on the New Jersey turnpike, listening to a newscast, I heard a band playing that anthem. Blood rushed to my face. Only after a few moments did I become aware that it was not 1936, and this was not a Nazi anthem anymore. I'd been listening to the news coverage of President Reagan's visit to Germany. Then, just a few days ago on the Autobahn, I heard the same tune again, and once more I forced away visions of Nazis in the Hitler salute.

And now I heard the tune live for the first time in all these decades, and still I saw Nazis in my eyes. I recalled my own terrible secret that I had shared only with Norman: that over the years, I myself would sometimes hum *"Deutschland über Alles,"* silently, in my mind, against my will. Was it what psychologists call "identification with the aggressor," I'd wondered? I didn't think so. "But a good example of the horrible ambivalence," Norman had observed.

Suddenly I realized the song had new words. I'd been so preoccupied with my flashbacks, I hadn't heard them. Still, the last two words left me uneasy—*"Deutsches Vaterland"* ("German fatherland"). Germany cannot possibly be the fatherland of any Jew! And yet, it was in fact once my homeland.

Yes, I am struggling with a horrible ambivalence, I reflected. I cannot be a full part of this, and I cannot be apart from it. I've been an observer on this trip but also a participant. Germany is in me, I want to feel good about it, yet I can't.

* * * * *
20

Don't They Know We Can't Forget?

O<small>N SATURDAY</small>, Walt and I stayed in Speyer, and went on our separate ways. I enjoyed myself purchasing wonderful souvenirs and diet chocolates. Then I visited Mariele and the former salesladies from my parents' store.

Mariele had existed in my mind over the years more as a piece of family lore than as a real person, a character in a story I'd pieced together from my family's conversations and from the old family album. In 1983, this legendary character had come to life.

Now, on the way to visit her, I again recalled my astonishment when that gray-haired woman pulled up in front of me on her bicycle, cocked her head, and exclaimed in disbelief, "This is Egon?!" And I recalled my instant sense of kinship, and that she was the only one I kissed good-bye.

We wrote to each other after that brief reunion, and she invited me to stay at her house in 1985, but she became ill. When Walt and I had visited her at the hospital on Thursday, she told us how much she regretted the bad luck. She'd worked so hard on the millennial planning committee and now had to miss the festivities, and she wanted so much to spend time with me. Although she didn't appear seriously ill and was sitting up, she seemed reserved and I suppressed my questions.

Today, she was out of bed, planning to go home in a couple of days, so I didn't have to hold back. Besides, I came to realize that Mariele's reserve was not due to illness alone. She spoke with few words, articulately. And in this short visit, I learned that she had indeed played a central role in my childhood.

"My parents worked constantly in the fields," she explained, "and from my earliest years I spent lots of time at your grandparents' house. I was nine years old when you were born. I looked after you, washed your diapers."

"Did my mother really bring me home in a basket on the *Pfefferminzbähnel*?" I asked.

"I don't know if it was in a basket," she chuckled, "but the only way from Speyer to Schwegenheim was by train." She used to ride with me on that little train too, she said, "and our faces would get black from the coal dust."

I continued to be amazed that with all that, I had remembered so little about her.

When I asked her about the woods and the *Hutzele*, she became more animated, almost gleeful. "Every Wednesday we would go. There were always many people with us, your grandmother, my mother, my sister, sometimes your mother. We put you in the handcart and took you along. We put the *Hutzele* into big sacks and carted them home to use for kindling. Even after your parents moved to Speyer, we sent them sacks full on the *Pfefferminzbähnel*. Your father would pick them up at the station."

As she talked about the millinery store, I got a fuller sense of the thriving business my mother and aunt had established in Schwegenheim long before they opened in Speyer. Three milliners worked for them in the village. Mariele fondly recalled how as a girl she would climb under the worktable and pick pins up from the floor with a magnet.

"I remember doing that too!" I exclaimed, using my hands to describe a horseshoe-shape magnet.

Mariele said she started working in the store in Speyer in 1932, at age 13. Then she told me something that completely surprised me. "I moved to Speyer and lived on Markusweg with you, on the third floor."

Though I had a room on that third floor I never recalled Mariele being up there. However, since I slept in my parents' room for quite a while, maybe by the time I moved to the third floor Mariele was no longer with us. If only she hadn't gotten sick, so that I could spend more time and ask these kinds of details!

When she told me she even went to synagogue with us every week and went with us on trips to Mannheim, I could hardly believe my ears. Mariele was practically part of the family, and I'd had no living memory of her. "I never realized we were together that much," I finally told her.

"When the Nazis came into power it got bad for all the Jews," she told me. "The store windows were sometimes smeared and postered with anti-Jewish slogans, the people were warned not to buy from and not to work for the Jews. But I stayed with you till the end."

"Didn't the Nazis bother you for that?" I asked.

"Only that the German Girls League would not accept me. After you left for America, I continued to work in the store for the new owners," she went on. "And I continued to see your grandparents every day. During the midday break I went across the Postplatz to visit them on Mühlturmstrasse."

As I listened to her and looked into her eyes, I believed her. But there was a voice of doubt inside me. The voice may have been that of my mother or Aunt Selma: *Yes, yes, even Mariele distanced herself from us!* I couldn't be sure. But another voice inside me said we'd have to forgive her, for Mariele, too, had to protect herself in those dangerous times.

At the end of the visit I told her, "Of all the people I met in Schwegenheim and Speyer, you seem to have been the closest. Now I know why you looked like a long-lost relative when I saw you in 1983."

She laughed. "Well, we weren't kin, but I was very close with you and your family."

As I walked out of the hospital I breathed in deeply, with that sense of freedom one feels when something clears up that had been stirring in the mind for a long time. I also felt an undefined tension but quickly dismissed it. My mind was on my next visits.

* * * * *

Mrs. Sold talked plaintively, often holding back tears. "When I saw in the paper about your visit," she exclaimed, "I knew immediately I had to see you, and rushed over to the newspaper to find out how I could contact you. And I immediately called Margaret, who is coming here in the car later—we thought it would be easier on your time that way—and Maria Wilkens, whose house you'll be going to. Oooh, oh my, ooh, how I remember your family, and how you used to come into the store as a boy and we girls would make such a fuss over you."

As Mrs. Sold reminisced, her words were sometimes punctuated with a gasp of joyful emphasis, sometimes with a sob of sadness. "And Selmaaa—how well I remember her. Oh! You say she is still living! Oh, you must tell her that you saw me. She will remember me—Betty Sold."

"My Aunt Selma was very fun-loving, wasn't she?" I asked.

"Oh my, yes was she ever fun-loving."

"And tell me about my parents," I said.

My mother was a hard worker, she explained, my father was more on the strict side but good-hearted. "We all got along like a family."

As she looked at my relatives in the photo album, she commented, "We all often wondered why they never wrote."

"They wrote to no one after they left," I said. "No one."

"Oh, yes. I know," she said, thoughtfully. "Of course I know. It was a bad time." She paused. "But it is over and we are still alive. Yes, yes, and I am so glad you came to see me."

She left the room and brought back a handful of pictures, one of herself inside the store she had opened after the war, and pictures of a group of young women taken in the woods somewhere in 1931. They had all worked in the store, she explained, pointing herself out. Then she pointed to Margaret.

"I recognize her!" I shouted, astonished, seeing the smiling friendly face that even now seemed to reach out to me. It was an eerie sensation, this sudden rebirth of a person buried in childhood's unconscious. "And when I show these pictures to Aunt Selma," I said, "she will let out a scream."

Mrs. Sold took a pen, and with tears in her eyes, slowly saying each word aloud, she wrote on the back of a photo: "Many, many regards to Selma." She started to cry. "I told myself I wouldn't cry," she said, touching my hand. "But I can't help it."

The doorbell rang. It was Margaret's husband. Although she was completely paralyzed on one side and hardly able to get around, he explained, she had pleaded with him to bring her, despite the pouring rain. She was waiting in the car.

I will never forget the heart-warming twenty minutes in that car, with the rain pelting the roof and rolling down the windows in rivulets.

"I just had to see you," Margaret started, her voice trembling. "We were told you wouldn't have time for too many visits so I decided that I had to get out to see you. One has to have some pleasures toward the end of one's life."

Margaret explained that she'd started working for my parents as soon as they opened their first Speyer store in 1928. In 1931, she was married.

I had a sudden flashback. I was walking into the Dom, with my mother holding my hand. She was nervous about going into a church, but it was for a wedding, she said.

"Did you get married in the Dom?" I asked Margaret.

She nodded.

"My mother brought me to your wedding!"

Margaret asked her husband to hand me "the photographs." To my utter astonishment, one was a picture of me in a *Fastnacht* (Shrove Tuesday) costume, similar to the one in my album, but this one showed my pale Germanic face with a most impish expression. I wore a hat with fringes cut into its huge brim, a cowboy outfit with matching fringes jutting out from the seams of the pants, a sash around my waist, a neckerchief around my neck and shoulders, and in my hand a long wooden pop-gun pointing at the camera. "This is a wonderful picture," I said, showing her the other one. "A wonderful companion photo."

As we said good-bye, I saw that she wanted to kiss me but could not lean over. "And tell Selma that you saw me," she pleaded, as I kissed her. "She will remember—Margaret, from the store."

* * * * *

My next visit, with Mrs. Wilkens, contained a memorable touch of humor, a surprising piece of new information about Aunt Selma, and some poignant political comments. We met at the home of her daughter, Mrs. Beisel, an articulate woman in her midforties. Mrs. Wilkens had a deep robust voice and an amusing way of expressing definite opinions.

"My mother was known in your family's store as 'Miss Maria,'" Mrs. Beisel started, at which Mrs. Wilkens threw her head up and laughed throatily, "Not 'Miss'! but 'Mrs. Maria!' Selma used to call me 'Miss' until finally when I was six months pregnant I had enough of it and told her not to illegitimize my child by calling me Miss."

Mrs. Beisel smiled and rolled her eyes, "You will have to forgive my mother; she is often outspoken with her feelings."

"And I taught you well," Mrs. Wilkens snorted with a husky, lighthearted laugh.

"Well yes. I am honest too," Mrs. Beisel said.

"Good. We will all be honest." I chuckled.

My mother was good to work for, Mrs. Wilkens continued, and my father was strict but a good man. "But Selma, she was a ruckus raiser!"

When I expressed surprise, Mrs. Wilkens said "Oh yes. *Ein Luder,*" which I figured out meant "a wretch."

"My Aunt Selma, a wretch? That's hard for me to believe," I said.

"Oh yes. That was a known fact," Mrs. Wilkens laughed.

"I told you, my mother is outspoken, Mr. Stern," Mrs. Beisel said.

"Listen," Mrs. Wilkens shot back. "He asked me to tell him honestly about his family, and that's what I'm doing.

"We girls worked from seven to eleven in the morning and then from one to seven. At five minutes to seven, Selma would give us another hat to make. And it would take an hour. So, once when Mr. Stern gave me my pay envelope I told him, 'My statement is incorrect.' He asked, 'How is that?' Then I said to him, 'I worked seven hours overtime.' Then when he confronted Selma, you should have heard her fight with him! My, how often those two would quarrel."

When Selma and her husband opened the store in Kaiserslautern, she explained, they asked her to work there. She didn't want to, but my mother told her, "Maria, don't be afraid of her. You know how to talk up for yourself." So she went.

My mind reached back to the family feuds in New York, and I recalled that indeed Aunt Selma could be pretty controlling at times. But a "wretch"? That I couldn't believe. In any case, I now better understood why my mother and her sister were often on the outs with each other long after we came to America. I had always thought it was my nervous mother who caused those rifts. But now I realized that I'd seen only Aunt Selma's affectionate side and her fun and games, not her tough side—in fact, I now also recalled that she used to be pretty hard on my cousin Bernie.

As Mrs. Beisel went to the kitchen to get cake and coffee, she said to her mother, "Tell Mr. Stern about the *Pfefferminzbähnel.*"

"Oh yes, our little train," Mrs. Wilkens said affectionately. "I sometimes traveled to the villages on it, and to Neustadt. It was so slow; we used to call it the *Bimbelbähnel.*"

"*Bimbelbähnel?*" I asked, puzzled. Bimbel sounds like a tinkle-bell, I reflected.

"*Bimmelbahn,*" Mrs. Beisel said, putting coffee cake on the table. "It means slow train, or local train."

"*Bimbelbähnel,* we called it," Mrs. Wilkens insisted. "And I was so sad when they took it away."

"We all were," Mrs. Beisel said.

"It holds some very dear memories for me too," I said. "And sad feelings."

"With your memories, and all that you are trying to find out, these must be strenuous days for you here in Germany," Mrs. Beisel said.

"It makes me happy being here, but sometimes it has been a strain," I admitted. "Quite a strain sometimes."

As we looked at the old photos of my parents' store, Mrs. Wilkens remarked that after we left, she didn't get along with the new owner. "Political conflict," Mrs. Beisel added. "Yes, political conflict," Mrs. Wilkens said. "The new owner wanted us to say 'Heil Hitler' to the customers. Not only that, he wanted us to accept the Nazi philosophy. When I refused, he got on my back, so one day I confronted him with something. He denied it, so I told him to go to hell, and I quit. Then he came to my apartment to tell me I wasn't allowed to make hats there. And I told him, 'You better leave or I'll throw you down the stairs!'"

"I thought that everybody was for Hitler," Mrs. Beisel said, "Or at least paid their dues to the party."

"Not so," Mrs. Wilkens shot back.

Mrs. Beisel turned to me. "Mr. Stern, I wasn't born till 1939. And we younger people, my generation, we see Hitler as a historical phenomenon. And we feel that one cannot undo what happened or make it over. And I want to tell you something more. I hope you don't mind. We said we could speak honestly."

"Please do," I assured her.

"Five years ago, Israel's Prime Minister, Begin," she began. "That Begin came to Germany and wouldn't shake our president's hand. We think that fuss Begin caused was unnecessary. It isn't a real issue today anymore. That Begin, he was an old fanatic, and he sowed so much hatred again. No, we young people could not identify with him."

Mrs. Wilkens chortled, "He sure shook hands when our President Schmidt gave him those millions."

"We young people," said Mrs. Beisel, "wouldn't want something like Hitler to ever happen again, but it wasn't our fault. We resent being always put on the carpet for it."

I started to say how hard it is for Jews to forget. "It is difficult. . . ."

"No." she interrupted. "It is not difficult. If both sides want to. And we want to. We want peace. And I think you want it too, Mr. Stern. I can see that."

"We didn't want a war," Mrs. Wilkens said. "No. My husband was killed. And my brother."

There was a silence. I groped again for words to explain how difficult it is for Jews to forget and come to complete peace with

Germany. "These things are complex . . . ," I began. "When we read the papers . . . we don't get the full picture. I myself try to be rational, but it's not easy for me to forget either, though I didn't suffer like others, but I had relatives killed. . . . Many, even those like me who were not in the camps, can't so easily forget."

"I understand," Mrs. Beisel nodded.

"And I also don't think everyone in Germany was a Hitlerite," I added. But afterwards I wondered: was that really so?

* * * * *

Exhilarated from these extraordinary meetings, I returned to the hotel and lay down to rest, but felt a swelling tide of distress.

I began rambling into my tape recorder: Everyone so warm, so friendly. . . . They reminisced with me over my childhood pictures. . . . Incredible that an old woman who couldn't walk would struggle to come to see me, in the rain, and bring pictures of me and my family, of Jews; they had saved the pictures despite the Nazis. . . . I'm glad I came back to Germany, even though others told me they wouldn't set foot on this soil. I understand why they can't, yet how long should we carry the grudge? Like some Germans said: "Our bread is buttered with it," "We young people resent being always put on the carpet for the past," "It wasn't our doing," "Begin didn't shake Schmidt's hand."

But don't they know we can't forget?! Don't they know what a horrible, horrendous thing it was? No, they don't! They can't. They didn't go through it. They don't study it, don't stare it in the face like I do. Even many Jews themselves can't stare it in the face—Milly can't watch a Holocaust film.

They want peace, they said. I want it too, more than anything. I've said it to Germans myself. We need peace more than ever to deal with dangers we face today: the nuclear threat, global pollution.

The way they all talk none of them supported Hitler. I'm sure that not everybody did; but not one person I've talked to said "I didn't vote for him." Oh yes, I can understand when they say, "He made jobs, and the people voted for him." And they Heil Hitlered too, I'm sure! Oh, I know intellectually why: they would have been jailed, beaten, shot. Yet not one person said to me, "I'm sorry I voted for him." But is that what I came to Germany for? For apologies? Did I expect them to get down on their hands and knees? Besides, some did express regret, sincerely—the young man at the pool, the mayor of Speyer, the man at the banquet.

How devoted everybody felt to the Peppermint Train! How friendly even every stranger had been! But I can't stop thinking about the camps. Can we forget the murders? No, Jews can never forget.

I stepped into the shower. The gushing water pelting my body excited my emotions to a higher pitch. "Why does talking with Germans make me feel so good, but also upset?" I shouted. Tears joined the water streaming down my face. "Because it brings out my attachment, and my hurt," I screamed. "I can't feel one without the other!

"But I didn't suffer like a survivor. So why do I feel so upset? Why am I agonizing so? *Because* I didn't suffer like a survivor?"

If another catastrophe befell the Jews, would the world again stand by? Has the world learned anything from the Holocaust? And what about the oppressions and massacres of other peoples?

"Your wife is Jewish too?" "But she's a nice person." And this morning, that young woman in the store, lamenting to another woman that she was referred to a specialist in Mannheim and found out he's a Jew. What should she do, she asked her companion. The companion told her to go to someone else.

Was I mishearing things? I've misheard things like that before.

My stupid statement at the radio show—Schwegenheimers always friendly, through darker times—I was rewriting history!

Knowing *why* things happened doesn't quench the anger. Maybe that's what I'm doing over and over again—shedding tears that many years ago I did not shed, shouting screams I did not shout. Maybe these last few days I wanted to shout in their faces. But the faces were so human, so kind.

Norman said it well: "You go there expecting to find monsters; in fact, you almost want to meet somebody that will justify your rage." Well, I found no monsters, but I did hear some profoundly disturbing things—some of them may not even have been said or meant the way I heard them. But if I hadn't heard them, I wouldn't have justification for my anger and my hurt. And maybe if we stopped being angry and hurt we would imply forgiveness? Or we might too readily forget?

I stepped out of the shower blowing a gutteral sigh from my mouth, "huchchsh," like a final hiss from a steam engine.

I felt calmer, but when Walt came in I had to ask him what he thought about the use of the word *Judde*.

He pointed out what I already knew—that although the term could be used in a derogatory way, it could also be a colloquialism. "But what about the lady who said, 'From the Jews?'" I argued.

"It's descriptive, the way people everywhere use the color of one's skin, or religion, or nationality. Even in America you might say 'the Indian woman,' 'the red-headed guy,' or 'the Jewish guy.'"

"Agreed," I said. "But don't you have any reservations at all about Germans, or Germany?"

"You're very sensitive to any sign of anti-Semitism," he said. "You have heartfelt feelings of resentment and feelings about the people that were associated with your memories, that I don't have. I think I'm more removed, I don't know what the word is, objective, or whatever."

"Maybe you don't see what I see," I argued.

"I think you want me to *feel* the way you do. But I can only go on my experience, and when I was here in 1982 and again this year, I was treated very well, warmly. You see things from your own experience, and maybe you are right; maybe I don't see what you pick up. Reading and learning about how the Germans treated the Jews can make me think about the things that were wrong but not necessarily to feel them."

"But what about the sense of horror I tried to instill in you and Debbie and Karen?"

"As I said before, the horror was cerebral. What was instilled in me was the emotional connection to German people and culture. We were raised in a family with a German feeling. Oma and Opa, Aunt Selma and Uncle Eugene and your other relatives all had German accents and sometimes spoke German.

And I heard stories about Germany. And don't you remember? You gave us German lessons when we were little. And then I studied German in high school. The more I learned the language and the culture, the more I liked it."

Yes, he's right, I thought. Walt had to remind me of the obvious. I never fully rejected my German heritage. I passed it on to my children. "I think I've been too hard on you," I finally said. Though I couldn't share his objectivity, I told him, I couldn't expect him to share my ambivalence.

"That's what I've been trying to tell you," Walt sighed.

We sat looking at each other, thoughtfully and with affection. Walt broke the silence. "Maybe it's time to take a break from this agonizing. How about if you rest while I shower? Remember, this is my night to take you out, to a restaurant of your choice."

"I've chosen the Ratskeller!" I said. "It's peaceful there, and the food is wonderful."

While resting, I recalled the wonderful German foods my mother used to cook—*Wienerschnitzel, Spätzle, Streuselkuchen*. Yes, I reflected, I cannot love Germany, but there are some things about my heritage I can truly appreciate, even love.

* * * * *

21

Das Pfefferminzbähnel

ON SUNDAY MORNING over coffee, we told Otto and Gisela about our wonderful Saturday of shopping in Speyer.

I explained that, most of all I had wanted an anniversary clock. From childhood on I'd been fascinated by those clocks with their rotating brass pendulums and spheres, and I would now finally have one of my own—from Germany. However, after much searching, I found a different kind of clock altogether. I fell in love with it immediately: a picture clock of an early steam locomotive with a coach, constructed of tiny silver and gold-colored objects—safety pins, hinges, gears and washers, tacks, sequins. Even smoke billowed from the chimney of the locomotive. It was my Peppermint Train—a clock that encapsulated the theme of this entire pilgrimage.

Later, Otto took us for visits with other former neighbors, including tours of the *Eckhaus* and my grandparents' former house. Our hosts were cordial, and eager to help, but the tours had less impact on me than I'd expected; they were anticlimactic to the many things I had already seen and learned.

Then Otto took us to the fairgrounds. As we sat sipping beer at one of the tables, Walt and I commented about the friendly, warm reception we had experienced in Germany. Otto nodded, but I sensed a certain hesitation in his expression. He was glad that we were enjoying our trip, he said, and that people were so friendly. Then he paused, took another sip of beer, looked aside as if uncertain about saying more. Finally he looked at me intensely. "I've been meaning to tell you something very frankly. It's important." Otto's intense look deepened. "I've been wanting to say this to you for three days: Fifty years ago the people in Germany did not talk the way they talk to you now."

"You mean . . ." I started.

"Many people you talked to talked very different about the Jews years ago," he blurted.

"Differently," I followed.

"Differently about the Jews that were taken away," he said, shaking a finger.

"I suspected so," I said, noddingly slowly.

His voice rose, and he pounded his fist on the table. "And I consider that a very big falsehood."

"They went along with the prevailing philosophy," I probed.

"And worse," he said, his eyes blinking furiously.

I had the urge to ask him to identify these people. But I didn't want to embarrass him. Besides, I probably didn't want to know. It might destroy my illusions of the goodness of those I met, even keep me from seeing them as ordinary human beings.

"All?" I hinted.

"No. Some."

"And Mariele?" I asked, carefully.

"Not Mariele," he said instantly. "She was not differently minded than she is today. She always acted on the same creed that I follow. In fact, she was the only one in the village who did not belong to the German Girls League. Someone even slapped her face for her beliefs." He sighed. "And that person is still alive."

I felt like asking who it was but didn't want to probe Otto too much. Or again, maybe I didn't really want to know.

"I could have asked this information of no one," I said.

"And no one would have told you," he said with finality.

"Now let me tell you a true story," Otto continued. "In

another village there was a man who had a very good Jewish friend. After Hitler came, that man persecuted his friend. He even had him arrested once. Despite this, the Jewish man came to visit the village after the war and went to greet his former friend. But that lousy man spat on him. That man was a totally dirty, foul, miserable human being, the foremost Jew-hater in his town. He is still alive." Then Otto whispered, "Now I want you to look, slowly, over there at the Frankfurter booth. That's him."

He was too far away for me to make out details, but I perceived an old man whose face was humorless and mean. He was tall, powerfully built, walking with a stoop and making eye contact with no one. I imagined him in a Nazi uniform, cracking a whip, cursing at Jews. And I visualized him spitting at his former friend.

"If I could only go over and spit at *him*," I whispered.

We sat pensively for a while and then went to the photo exhibition. I felt a burst of pleasurable surprise when, among the hundreds of photos and snapshots dating as far back as the 1800s, was a photo of Aunt Selma as a young woman, next to Uncle Leon. Again, my thought was: Germans saved pictures of their Jewish friends, despite the Nazis.

Then my eyes stopped at another photo—this time with shock. A column of boys was shown marching down a street. They appeared to be wearing the brown shirts, shorts, and ties of Hitler uniforms, and they carried fifes and drums. One carried a big flag. The leader flourished a baton, his other hand resting imperiously on his big belt buckle. *A Nazi parade!* I screamed, silently.

Conscious of the many people around me, I tried to hide my emotions but nevertheless crouched down for a closer look. The furrows in my forehead deepened. Through the folds of the big flag, I detected part of a swastika. It couldn't be, I thought. Maybe they're Boy Scouts. But those words written below the photo, "*Spielmannzug von Schwegenheim bei der Musterung.*" What do they mean? Yes, it must be a military muster, an enrollment, a review.

To my relief, I found no other photos commemorating that aspect of village history. How did that one sneak in? I wondered.

When I ran into the mayor, I had regained enough composure to ask him to autograph my Schwegenheim anniversary book. As we shook hands to say good-bye, he said, "And now Mr. Stern, I must tell you something. I really want to express my sorrow about what was done to your people, including the deeds of many town mayors." I detected tears in his eyes.

* * * * *

The parade was grand, with dozens of floats and marchers depicting one thousand years of village life, from farm to battlefield: wheat threshing, tobacco and peppermint processing, barrel making and weaving, timber cutting in "The Schwegenheimer Woods," oxen, goats with authentic wooden farm carriages, displays of cheese making, chicken raising, ancient cavalry, Roman chariots in battle dress, an early fire engine and a modern one on which they poured beer from fire extinguishers. The crowd laughed heartily at a float on "child rearing," consisting of a two-story-high twin-headed stork, followed by little girls pushing ancient wicker baby carriages.

"Here comes the *Pfefferminzbähnel,*" Gisela said, as we heard a whistle and the clang of a bell from up the street, and then the sound of "Sh, sh, sh, sh."

I had fantasized a genuine locomotive, spumes of steam, a chimney sending smoke into the air, coaches with people peering out of windows, maybe even a conductor punching tickets. But what came down the street was a model. No smoke, no steam, its sounds electronic, except for the bell, to which my heart reached out. But it was a wonderful imitation of my train. The locomotive's black iron wheels were painted on a red frame that rode just inches from the ground, leaving barely visible the rubber tires from the truck bed onto which the whole structure was built. There was a black cab with an "engineer" inside, and a barrel-shaped engine housing from the front of which rose a cone-shaped black chimney. The cab had a convex black metal roof, giving it an authentic appearance.

The locomotive pulled three small wagons, like those one rides on a boardwalk, and I gleefully tried jumping on to join the "passengers." A chain blocked my way, and the "conductor" ordered me off.

"But I am Egon Stern, and want to ride my train again!" I almost shouted.

As the float disappeared into the distance, I finally knew I would never again ride my Peppermint Train.

* * * * *

As soon as the parade ended, I set out alone for a last walk to my woods. I strolled briskly down Bahnhofstrasse, but at the edge of town I stopped. Do I really want to do this again? I asked myself. Didn't I have enough in 1983? But something compelled me on.

Dozens of people were streaming toward the woods, alone, in families, in groups, on foot, on bicycles, chatting, laughing, singing. But their happiness and the powerful sense of their togetherness saddened me. At home in America, my neighbor across the street said hello maybe five times in fifteen years.

The tears don't leave me alone, I noted. I'm pining for the sense of community I felt here as a little boy. I never realized it ran so deep. But are these tears also tears of anger?

At the path into the woods, I wavered again and started to turn back, when I saw a man on a bicycle heading toward me. I recognized him—Mr. Bein, Otto's eighty-three-year-old cousin from Gommersheim. He had come to the parade on his bike and was now riding home. "In America," I told him, "people would look in amazement at a man your age on a bicycle, especially riding such a distance. They ride cars for transportation."

"I don't even know how to drive a car," he laughed.

We said a warm good-bye, and I strode onto the path into the woods, continuing to talk to myself about good and evil, how little we know about the causes and prevention of mass slaughter. Then I fell silent, and I stood still, listening to the birds and the other gentle sounds of these lovely woods. I was surprised at what I blurted out next. "If I could, I would want to live here." But I quickly countered myself. "That can never be. I would not want it."

I imagined the clearing where little Egon sat on a blanket, a basket of yellow grapes in front of him, his caretakers gleefully gathering *Hutzele*. And although I knew in my head that it was pure fantasy to find that clearing, my heart turned me onto a trail to the left.

Instead of a clearing, I saw something that made me shudder: an all-metal, windowless trailer, all closed up except for a metal chimney. *Jews were gassed here!* I thought. *This is a mobile gas van!* I quickly came back to my senses, realizing that this little metal trailer could not have been a gas van, and in any case it wouldn't have been left here.

I took a deep breath, walked back to the main path, and again savored the delicious aromas of the woods, the soft sound of rustling of leaves, the songs of birds. I hiked down the path to the clearing that had been the route of the Peppermint Train. I sat down against a tree and closed my eyes, recalling all I had learned these last two years about the little *Pfefferminzbähnel*. Images started forming in my mind—maybe imaginary ones, maybe real ones that had been waiting to thaw from Egon's time-frozen memory.

I'd learned that the tracks were just a little more than a yard wide—forty inches, to be exact. To an adult that would be a really little train—maybe a sort of giant toy, a big model railroad. But to Egon, it must have looked lots bigger. What a change, between Egon's image and Edgar's—as I experienced at the parade today!

I imagine that little train excited many children like me, watching the locomotive jostle into the station, its cone-shaped chimney smoking, big iron whiskers dancing on the track. What multitude of fragrances wafted through the train's little windows as it meandered through fields and woods—delicious scents of trees and leaves and brush, sweet aromas of wildflowers and peppermint, pungent garlic, stink of cow dung. And when acrid black smoke poured through the windows, adults would close their eyes and pinch their noses, cough; some would complain and a few would denounce, and occasionally someone would be heard swearing; some would laugh, and some would chuckle and grunt all at the same time. Children would be pulled away from the windows, laughing, coughing, squirming, and stirring up a fuss, in the midst of which a young one could be heard screeching as its mother tried to dislodge a cinder from an eye with the corner of her handkerchief.

I imagine that no child ever rode that train without trying to stretch a little way out the window for an exciting view when it went around a curve. And would any parent not warn about the danger of hanging out too far? Nor can I imagine any child not begging to ride in the front car to watch the palpitating engine joggle and pull, to hear its shrill whistle and tinkly bell, and to await an eruption of steam from its belly and smoke from the funny-shaped stack.

That beloved train also intimidated a young, sensitive child like Egon with real and imagined dangers—dangers that adults didn't think about. Egon would be startled as the train quickly slowed or stopped, and if it stopped on a trestle and swayed, he'd worry lest it couldn't start up again. Egon experienced those fears—maybe even sought them—as excitement, thrills.

And as I rode the *Pfefferminzbähnel* in the fall, what splendorous splash of colors in those passing woods, what wondrous whifsf of foliage in its final stage of life! And in the winter, I would press my nose on the window pane, mesmerizing myself with a secret game of counting tree trunks, till my eyes would close.

As I slowly walked out of my woods, I knew I had come back today to say good-bye.

* * * * *

22

Dachau

"IN NO WAY CAN I justify visiting Germany this year without going to see a concentration camp," I had said, long before the trip, "no matter how much time and extra money it will take."

On Monday morning, during the long drive to Dachau, my reasons became clear. I needed to see with my own eyes one of those places where the ghastly deeds were committed. I need to see it for my relatives. I need to see it to appease my guilt for having escaped its horrors, to help reconcile my feelings.

"Dachau was one of the original concentration camps," I said to Walt. "The Nazis sent many people there for political and other reasons."

"Gisela said it was the place where everybody feared being sent if you didn't do what you were told," Walt remembered.

"It wasn't a mass death camp like Auschwitz," I reflected, "but I think it stands as a symbol of all concentration camps, the symbol of Nazi terrorism."

When we got off the Autobahn, the local road to Dachau was like any other pleasant little country road, but in my eyes it turned grayer and darker the closer we got to the town. The hamlets and villages we passed were like other pleasant old German communities, but I visualized them as passive bystanders to the infamous crimes that were committed nearby, bystanders to the trainloads of prisoners, to the torture and blood in the camp.

Although it was hardly past noon, I became irrationally concerned about how late it was getting, and found myself so obsessively worried about Walt taking a wrong turn that I navigated his driving.

"I know where I'm going. I've watched the signs," he would answer me with annoyance. "Stop worrying. If we don't see it today, we have all day tomorrow. That's why we allotted two days, to make absolutely sure we wouldn't miss Dachau."

"I'd like to get it over with today, then get the hell far away," I argued. "I don't think I could fall asleep in a hotel around here." Deep down I wondered if I would be able to sleep anywhere that night.

Shortly, I grimaced and my neck shrunk into my shoulders. "Slow down," I said in a cracked voice. "There's a sign: 'Concentration Camp Memorial Site.'"

"I see it," Walt snapped.

"It says turn left," I persisted.

"Okay, okay," he replied.

"I'm sorry," I apologized. "It's hot, and I'm tired."

"And anxious," he said.

The tall guard towers came into view, then the massive stone wall topped with menacing barbed wire.

As we walked from the parking lot to the present-day entrance gate, we found that the camp was closed on Mondays. Other visitors were also at the gate, disappointed.

The huge compound looked immense, boundless. A few wooden barracks stood in the center. They were obviously what remained of dozens, maybe hundreds more. There was a ditch all around the compound, at least ten feet deep. It was ringed by barbed wire. This was surrounded by another ring of barbed wire atop a stone wall.

"Let's go," I said. "We'll look for a place to stay outside of Dachau."

We found a small hotel in a nearby town. I felt calm now but solemn. Walt fell asleep, but I rested only briefly. When I saw a notice in a local paper about a pretzel fair in the next town, I felt that attending such an event would be totally inappropriate to the solemnity of my visit here. But I couldn't resist.

The cacophonous fair music grated against my gloom. I felt a pang of guilt for having come and walked to an adjacent quiet lake. As I sat staring at the water, the faint carnival music drifted on and off in a mild breeze, and I thought: During the war, I fiddled while millions burned. And here I come to a carnival. No, I can't divorce the ugly past—that's why I came to Dachau. But neither can I divorce the lovely past—that's why I came to the carnival. Maybe it was like going to the Messplatz to attend the Speyer fair again.

The next morning, hundreds of visitors streamed into the camp. By bus, by car, by bicycle they came. They spoke different languages, many of them English. There were many, many Germans, including busloads of schoolchildren.

The orientation film explained that Dachau is the living symbol for all other camps run by the Nazis. Just as I had thought. What I had not known was that there were hundreds of such camps all over Germany. Dachau was merely the largest and best known.

Surprisingly, though I was somber, I did not feel the horror I had expected to feel. In fact, my mood was neutral. Maybe it was the presence of so many people. Maybe I was cried out. Maybe I had reconciled something. Had I settled some of my feelings?

As the film continued, my neutrality broke down. When Hitler's strident gravelly voice ranted, my spine stiffened and the blood tingled in my head. When starved prisoners were paraded on the campgrounds and beaten, I could hardly look, and alternately closed and opened my eyes. I forced myself to keep them open though the medical experiments, through the piles of human bones.

In the memorial hall exhibit, even the children uttered hardly a sound. And when we came out, Walt remarked that the exhibits intensified, concentrated, and focused the atrocities for him. He was dismayed at the range of prisoners: not just Jews but Christians, Communists, homosexuals, gypsies, and others. And while he had known this, seeing that each group wore their own identification badges drove the point home. Most of all, Walt said, he was amazed by the detailed records the Nazis kept—formal protective-custody letters, long family and personal background forms. "So much bureaucratic red tape is incongruous, considering that ultimately most died," he said. "But it amplifies how deliberate the whole process was."

At Dachau I saw for the first time with my own eyes the black wrought-iron subterfuge that greeted the millions as they entered the death camps: *ARBEIT MACHT FREI.* "Work Makes Free" was the ingenious motto that kept the hideous secret even from those that were about to be slaughtered. I saw with my own eyes the tiered bunks where the living dead had lain. Against my will, their pitiful bulging eyes inside sunken cheeks now looked straight at me. At me, who had never suffered.

I saw with my own eyes the ovens. And against my will I saw Aunt Anna and Lydia.

* * * *
23

I Know Now

"THE ONLY GOOD German is a dead German."

The words shocked me. They were spoken by Holocaust survivors, in a discussion group I attended shortly after my 1985 trip. "The discussion leader was a therapist like us," I told Milly. "With all her professional insight, she too said that the only good German is a dead German."

"Wishing a whole people dead is doing exactly what the Nazis did," Milly observed.

"Genocidal wishes, from Jews who themselves were survivors of genocide," I added.

"Did everybody in the discussion group agree?" Milly asked.

"No. In fact, one woman told me that she doesn't attend many of those meetings because they're so full of anger and hatred."

That night I asked myself, was it the rage of those survivors that troubled me, or did they stir up my own lingering mistrust of Germans? Despite my wonderful memories of German woods, of the Peppermint Train, I still felt anger about Uncle Arthur, Aunt Anna, Cousin Lydia, and the millions of others—sorrow and anger about Dachau and all concentration camps.

And if I, who never experienced the horror of the camps, can't let go of my anger, what can I expect survivors of those camps to feel? How I raged about merely being kicked out! Might I, too, wish all Germans dead if I had starved on a piece of bread and a bowl of thin soup, if I had seen my mother and father machine-gunned at the edge of a ditch or had smelled the ovens in which they burned?

"I am totally unforgiving of past Germans, present Germans, and Germans one hundred generations to come," said Sol, a survivor I talked with in 1987. "Near my home town in Latvia, 100,000 were buried in a mass grave. My parents and sister may have been among them. My wife's parents were also murdered at the hands of the Germans. Ed, how could you possibly set foot on German soil?"

I told him about the sorrow and anger I experienced in my visits, the powerful attachments that had been reawakened, and my continuing struggle to find answers. "We have to go beyond emotion in order to understand why it happened, in order for the Holocaust to serve as a lesson for humanity," I said.

"My feelings will never change!" he answered.

"Sol blames the children for the sins of their fathers," I told Milly later. "But considering what he went through I shouldn't blame him for his hatred."

"But neither should you blame yourself for your attachment and love," Milly reminded me.

"You know," I said, "I've talked to survivors who don't feel hatred, although they suffered as much as Sol did."

"There are times when we all want others dead," said Milly.

"That's not the same as racial hatred," I replied. "I don't think I've ever wished a whole people dead, not even the Germans during the war." But I recalled my murderous rage at individuals—the driver who tailgated me on the New Jersey Turnpike in 1984, the vile ex-Nazi Otto pointed out in 1985. I have lots of aggression in me, too. "Maybe it's true, what I've read—that most of us, given certain circumstances, would override our moral, religious, and social prohibitions and become violent. Or stand passively by while others do."

"To protect myself and my family I probably would have

obeyed the Nazis. At least I wouldn't have actively resisted them," Milly admitted.

"Others have told me the same thing," I observed. "But if I actually committed a violent act, I should be held responsible even if anyone else in my shoes might have done the same thing. Responsibility and guilt don't change merely because of circumstances or human nature."

The questions that had begun to plague me when I first started thinking about going back to Germany eight years ago were still there. I had come to realize that the urge to make that first trip had plunged me into a personal crisis from which I had not yet emerged.

Indeed, as I continued to look at my past, as I stared the Holocaust in the face, as I wrote and rewrote my story, I was sometimes struck with overwhelming pangs of anger, sadness, and guilt. I cried about the day I left my grandparents in Speyer, I rued my failure to appreciate my father, I mourned those who had perished.

My dreams expressed some of my most troubling feelings. In one nightmare, I found myself in an area that looked like a camp. I saw three live stick figures—each a heavy, black broomstick with a spindle for a head around which was woven thin, grey hair. The pitiful creatures held their heads sideways, tried to come toward me, but then warily kept their distance. They looked like grotesque living dead, waiting expectantly to be petted or fed. I felt sorry for them and wanted to comfort them, but I too kept my distance.

"I could have been them!!" I screamed as I awoke, trying at the same time to shake a horrible feeling that I *wanted* to be them. The dream brought me face to face with my guilt for having survived, and guilt over the distance I had kept from my feelings about the Holocaust.

As my mind focused on the violent times my family and I had lived through, everyday troubles paled in significance. I began to feel ridiculous worrying about a scratch on my car, a weed in my lawn. Even the sufferings of my patients often seemed trivial in comparison to the cosmic events that preoccupied me. Isn't there something bigger I can do to help this world? I asked myself.

As I thought about my anger, about the rage and racial hatred of survivors, I became increasingly aware that for many people the Holocaust perverted all that is dear. When we face the fact that "civilized" people can commit such horrendous evil, some of us lose trust in our fellow human beings, our institutions, in God. Many camp survivors became bitterly obsessed with their traumatic experiences. For me, the specter of the trains to the camps tainted my view of my dear Peppermint Train. Indeed, had I survived a journey on one of those death trains, all good feelings for my innocent little train might have been obliterated. As it was, I had nearly obliterated all memory of the simple pleasures of my childhood.

Yet, finally, I had to ask myself: Is it not a further perversion of my values to be unable to forgive? Can't I, like Lore and Aunt Helene, say that Eichmann had some good in him because he gave Uncle Willie cigarettes? I could not. What vile human being did not during his life make some charitable little gesture? I suspect that Lore and Aunt Helene needed to tell the cigarette story to help them to continue to live among Germans. In order to go on, they needed to screen out some unendurable truths and place a mist over the most painful episodes of the past.

I put the question to my family one day: "Can we, should we, forgive?"

"Your cousin David said 'Forgive but never forget,'" Walt reminded me.

"That's become a rather popular phrase recently," I replied. "But the dictionary defines 'forgive' as ceasing to feel resentment, absolving, pardoning, granting relief from wrongs committed."

I thought for a moment, then continued. "It's exactly our resentment that makes us remember. Then too, maybe it's easier to forgive someone if they repent. Not just by asking to be forgiven, but by actively doing something. Like taking schoolchildren to visit Dachau. That's what the Germans should do—study their past and contribute to the world's understanding of what happened."

"You're still as obsessed with trying to find answers as

you were after you returned from your first trip in 1983," my brother-in-law Norman observed.

"Anger and hatred won't help us understand," I said. "And if we don't understand, how can we prevent another Holocaust?"

If the circumstances of the 1930s were to present themselves again, I asked, would the world act any differently? What lessons have we learned from Germany, from the other countries who supported the Holocaust, and from those, including America, who wouldn't lift a finger to rescue the Jews? What lessons have we learned from Hiroshima? Unless we learn from those events, I declared, we are doomed as a species on this earth.

"Do you really think we can ever *understand* the Holocaust?" Norman asked. "You tell us about some very moving things. Then you speak of finding lessons from the Holocaust. You mean like in a quiz, Ed? You tell us about these moving things and then you say that you don't want to be ruled by your emotions.

"You're agonizing about not understanding," he continued. "But I offer you this paradox: Imagine an event of such great horror that it is beyond human comprehension. And those who come after feel that, for whatever reason, they absolutely must understand. And the more they try to make sense of it, the more they try to fit it into the scope of human comprehension, the more they trivialize it. And the sooner they forget. I think we will have to ritualize the remembering and forswear the understanding."

"In other words, we can't change the human condition?" I questioned. "We can't fight the power of hatred and prejudice? We can't eliminate, or even reduce, mass slaughter? In other words, the Holocaust has not been a lesson for mankind?"

"Has it?"

"But Norm, I'm troubled by your saying we should stop trying to understand," I continued. "The Holocaust has raised, more clearly than any other historical event, the most fundamental questions about the human condition. We have a responsibility to try to learn from it. As long as we keep trying we may make little bits of progress. Ritualizing the remembering is not enough. We must also ritualize the search for understanding. We ought to have more courses in our schools. We should discuss the Holocaust at our Passover Seders instead of merely retelling the story of leaving Egypt two thousand years ago."

Nevertheless, after that discussion I felt a sad sense that my hopes for a wiser, more humane world were futile, a sense that other Dachaus will be created: that out of our aggressive and genocidal impulses and our sociopolitical imperatives, millions of future lives will be traumatized and lost.

Then I had another revealing dream. Somewhere in Europe I was standing around a huge crater. My father and a few other people stood next to me. Suddenly the edge of the crater started moving. I thought I was the only one who saw it move. It moved outward, foot by foot, and was about to swallow us. Then my father shouted, "Back, back!"

The nuclear crater! Some day it may swallow us all. But the dream had a profound meaning, too. It was my father who saved me from being swallowed up by the Holocaust. It was he who insisted we come to America, far away from the Nazis. The dream reminded me that it wasn't just large questions about the human condition that had been troubling me. I'd been struggling with emotional questions about myself and my family, especially my father. That's really why I went back to Germany in the first place.

And I had gotten to know my father in a way I never had before. I was able to see how deeply our different personal stresses had strained our relationship. Not until now had I understood the profound trauma my father had suffered—the loss of his relatives, the loss of his dreams of personal success. It was only since visiting Germany that I had understood my own losses, and my struggle for acceptance in a new culture: how often I had scorned my father's German accent, especially after I had so quickly shed my own; how I strove to be a champion speller in English; how I yearned to have American friends, yet found myself mostly with my German-Jewish buddies; how I pleaded one day with my parents for an American winter jacket after other boys had taunted me for wearing a long overcoat—and then how I loved my new American pea jacket!

No, I haven't found answers to the cosmic questions about the Holocaust that some of the world's finest scholars are still struggling to resolve. Despite the explanations put forth from every possible perspective—historical, sociopolitical, psychological, moral, and so on—the Holocaust remains incomprehensible to me and to many others. Although I continue to study the "explanations," I don't think I will ever understand the massacre of my relatives and millions of people.

But while I didn't find the answers I sought about the Holocaust, I did find some answers about myself. My journey into my German-Jewish childhood finally enabled me to mourn. I wept over the loss of my childhood surroundings, over my relatives and my people. I raged. I confronted my horrible ambivalence. And I don't hear the German national anthem in my head anymore.

I've become aware of how Egon's persecution had made him keenly self-conscious, sometimes paranoid, about being Jewish, and how that persecution had made him feel he had done something wrong, sometimes to the point of hating himself. And I know now that Egon was innocent, and that Edgar can be proud of being Jewish. And I know that I don't have to be ashamed of my German background either. In fact, when someone recently asked me what my middle initial stands for, for the first time I proudly said, "Egon."

Perhaps most of all, despite or because of a pessimistic outlook for a more peaceful world, I came away with a better appreciation of the importance of relationships between individuals, including personal relationships between Jews and Germans.

Although I still have mixed feelings about Germany, I've stayed in touch with the people I met with in 1985. I've sent annual holiday cards, and I've corresponded with Otto, Dr. Rosskopf, Mariele, and Emma. Otto is a steadfast friend who has sent me such things as a pine branch with *Hutzele*. One day I was thrilled to receive from him a cone-shaped cardboard hatstand from my parents' store.

Yes, it is more than all right to reestablish connections with Germans. Indeed, it is a responsibility. Germans, especially in the little towns, now see few if any Jews, and I would like to think that, for those I met, my appearance and my continuing contact keeps the past alive in a personal way, a way that no books or television shows can. As long as we have a dialogue, we can teach the lessons of the Holocaust. It is probably for that reason that I referred to Dachau when I wrote to Konrad and Klaus. Now I know that I didn't want them to think I was taking a pleasure trip to Germany in 1985! I wanted to be honest about my purpose. And if I should return to Germany, I may even ask bolder questions.

I know I can never again love my homeland. The torn connection can never be fully mended. But I continue to love my wonderful Peppermint Train and to cherish the happy memories of my German childhood. And I continue to live with the awareness of Dachau, of Auschwitz, of the six million.

Such a past hangs on.

Library of Congress Cataloging-in-Publication Data

Stern, Edgar E.
  The peppermint train : journey to a German-Jewish childhood / Edgar E. Stern.
    p.   cm.
    ISBN 0-8130-1109-4 (alk. paper)
    1. Jews—Germany—Biography. 2. Stern, Edgar E.—Childhood and youth. 3. Stern, Edgar E.—Journeys—Germany. 4. Jewish children—Germany—Biography. 5. Holocaust, Jewish (1939–1945)—Germany. 6. Germany—Biography. I. Title.
DS135.G5S739   1992   91-31150
940.53'18'092—dc20   CIP
[B]